FROM LARK RISE
TO MADISON COUNTY

FROM LARK RISE
TO MADISON COUNTY

Francis Key

Library of Congress Control Number:		2010914076
ISBN:	Hardcover	978-1-4535-8106-3
	Softcover	978-1-4535-8105-6
	Ebook	978-1-4535-8107-0

This book was printed in the United States of America.

To order additional copies of this book, contact:
Xlibris Corporation
1-888-795-4274
www.Xlibris.com
Orders@Xlibris.com
85939

CONTENTS

This book is dedicated to my family; my parents, sisters and brother and to all of the amazing people throughout the world who I was so privileged to have as friends . And it is especially dedicated to my wife and our five children and nine grandchildren of who I am so very proud. Thank each of you for being such wonderful sources of love, support and joy throughout my life.

INTRODUCTION

In the early 1960s, whilst I was still at school, my family relocated from industrial Sheffield to rural Oxfordshire. This semi-autobiographical writing begins in this unlikely setting and weaves its way back there via New Zealand, South Africa, Scotland, and darkest Alabama, USA.

The start of this journey was close to the birthplace of Flora Thompson in the area, which formed the background for her account of village life in North Oxfordshire at the turn of the twentieth century. *From Lark Rise to Candleford* was published in 1939. By 1960, as a newcomer to country life, it appeared to me that very little had changed. By contrast, it was abundantly clear that the New Zealand of 1983 did not know the meaning of the word *change,* and Alabama thought that it had, by its involvement in sending man to the moon, seen all the change that was healthy in one lifetime. South Africa, on the other hand, was possibly just awaking to the fact that the cosy life that the white minority had enjoyed for so long was about to end forever.

Madison County was not the one made famous by Robert James Waller in his book *The Bridges of Madison County*, but an entirely different place in North Alabama, the story of which had an entirely different and infinitely more satisfying outcome.

CHAPTER 1

BEGINNINGS

'What I want to know is why those brothel-bred bastards are still teachers this morning!'

So began Edgar Thomas's weekly hate session with his Sixth Form, and my introduction to my new school. As headmaster, or 'Master', as he preferred to be known of the fading pile known as Magdalen College School, he felt it necessary to point out the failings of most of mankind to the elite of his school, the majority of whom would soon, he somewhat optimistically anticipated, be eagerly picked up by the great universities of Oxford and Cambridge. Indeed, the only pupils that he deemed worthy of his serious attention were those who aspired to gain entry to those hallowed institutions.

This school was not the famed learning academy in the city of dreaming spires, but an all together less impressive establishment in the nearby rural backwater of Brackley, originally set up in the sixteenth century in order to evacuate pupils from Oxford where the plague was raging. As I listened to Edgar's diatribe, I certainly wished that someone had bothered to notice that the plague had ended rather a long time ago and then had the presence of mind to close the place down.

Edgar, not an especially large man, succeeded in filling the room (and indeed the entire school) with his dark presence. As a strong advocate and practitioner of corporal punishment, which he dispensed liberally with his cane, he was feared by teachers and pupils alike. What little charm he possessed he conserved carefully in order to be able to lavish it thickly upon visiting parents and potential benefactors. Most of us came to witness its excrescence over our own parents as he attempted to ingratiate himself to them, but he made no such overtures to us, his captive victims. He was not averse to begging for money, and then, having delivered his grovelling plea, savaging his audience. He did exactly this to the old students' association at their annual dinner one year, one minute oozing bonhomie and pleading for each of us to donate generously to our alma mater, the next berating us as if we were still under his charge. The reason for this was that he had discovered that recent leavers had smuggled a miniscule amount of beer into the school to provide transient relief to the remaining inmates.

The first target of his ire on this particular morning was the entire staff of the neighbouring secondary modern school, which, in a rare and misguided foray across the class barrier, had organised a joint sports day, during which two boys narrowly missed being impaled upon a javelin, and two others received serious injury, playing 'catch' with the shot. More to the point, Magdalen had, quite deservedly, been resoundingly beaten. This had never been part of Edgar's plan when he agreed that his school would take part in the 'damned thing' and such failure ought to have been averted, by fair means or foul, as far as he was concerned.

As Edgar's tantrum reached fever pitch, and he fiercely propelled his desk down its well-worn track along the centre aisle kick by kick, his new target became Fred, a pale, odious, individual who had recently applied to a local employer and benefactor of the school for a scholarship to aid his future studies, which were certainly much required. On being asked, at interview, what his hobbies were, he had replied 'bricklaying mate' and had thus, in the master's words 'pulled the plug on himself'. The correct way to have answered was, apparently, to the effect that he 'had an interest in the delicate and ancient art of bricklaying, in its many and varied forms.' This would have been an elegant response, albeit devoid of any vestige of truth. He then informed Fred that he 'deserved to be flayed to within an inch of his bloody life with red hot barbed wire' for this grievous lapse. Fred then mumbled something to the effect that, in any case he had changed his mind and was now applying for a job in a local bank. Edgar's hysterically delivered response was that this would suit Fred down to the ground as 'bloody banks take anything, as long as it moves and breathes'. If I managed to glean anything worthwhile from Edgar during my short sojourn at this ghastly school, it is this statement. It has provided me with great solace, particularly early in my career, when requesting support from financial institutions full of such individuals who usually delighted in feigning superiority and being as unhelpful as possible. One possibly endearing feature of Edgar's admonitions was his practice of ending each one with the phrase, 'Let that be an object lesson to you!' Clearly, these outbursts were an essential part of his teaching method.

Having demolished Fred, he then rounded, in his absence, upon the religious knowledge teacher, an altogether more satisfactory target as far as the class was concerned. It is always fun to see such a sanctimonious individual castigated, although this harmless, but rather ineffective, ex colonial, nicknamed 'Bwana,' certainly did not deserve Edgar's ire for the misdemeanour of simply having failed to find the time to read that morning's newspaper, but it did afford the rest of us respite from Edgar's withering scorn.

The early weeks of my short career at this school were confusing. Why was the name spelt 'Magdalen', but pronounced 'Maudlin', an altogether more accurate description of the school and its staff, whose main claims to fame were an Oxford or a Cambridge degree and a total lack of enthusiasm. The head of physics typified this to perfection, his idea of teaching being to condemn even the most exciting scientific discoveries of the age to an agonisingly slow death at his hands by lecturing for eternity in a dull monotone. Indeed, it was with considerable relief that I later learned that he had been prosecuted for kicking in the door of a car that he had found blocking the entrance to his driveway. At least, he was capable of this one primitive outburst of emotion.

Lunch was prefaced by standing to attention to listen to the master intone a Latin grace, which was the only civilised feature of the entire meal, but incomprehensible to those of us who were fortunate enough to have escaped the dictate of being forced to learn Latin. We pupils sat at tables that each accommodated twelve of us. Every table had students of a carefully calculated cross section of ages seated at it and was presided over by the most senior, usually an ignorant bully, who was responsible for dividing the food supplied to the table between its unfortunate occupants.

Inevitably, this individual usually ensured that his own hunger and that of his friends was well sated, leaving little for the younger or less popular of those around the table. How those who boarded at the school, and were totally at the mercy of this system for their sustenance, ever survived to maturity is a complete mystery. Presumably, the less palatable dishes of the week, shunned by all but the desperate, were extremely nutritious and served to keep those unfortunates at the bottom of the pecking order alive.

A further mystery was the game of rugby, in the first instance watching two mediocre teams knocking hell out of one another on a dull winter's afternoon from the touchline. The one comfort we afforded ourselves was to sit down only to be forced to our feet by the master's gowned presence approaching like some particularly malevolent eagle swooping ever closer to its prey, screeching 'stand up you spineless individuals'. This, however, was nothing compared with playing the game; no explanation of the rules, merely aggressive invitations to mutilate the opposition, and hence, put one's own safety at risk. This was not made any better by Edgar's shrieks of encouragement to the school team, such as, 'Rip his bloody arm off, and hit him with the soggy end!' My own introduction to actually playing the game was made all the worse by a stray dog, which knocked me off my feet whilst I was making a futile attempt to join in the general madness. This totally extinguished any vestige of enthusiasm that I may have had for the game. Why one was forced to waste one's Wednesday afternoons thus, and then make up the time by attending school on Saturday mornings was particularly hard for me to understand.

This whole experience contrasted deeply with that of my previous mixed ability school in the industrial north of England. This was run by a devout and kindly Methodist who led a dedicated team of young, enthusiastic teachers, who worked wonders in motivating their pupils. I still remember his reply when asked by a student whether it was preferable to study French or woodwork, 'Woodwork doesn't open doors!' This, of course, related to the requirement of having successfully studied a foreign language as a condition of entry into most colleges. Motivation failed on Speech Days, when we were expected to be inspired by singing the school hymn 'The Day Thou Gavest Lord is Ended'. To this day, I fail to find the stimulation demanded of this hymn, as a rallying call to young souls about to venture out into the world of adulthood. I can only assume that its choice was purely because it happened to be the headmaster's favourite hymn.

I was fortunate to attend this school early in its short life. Opened with great aplomb by Princess Margaret in 1953, even by the time of my arrival in the late fifties, ominous cracks were appearing in its structure. It was destined to be demolished very early on in the twenty-first century. If only Magdalen had been so poorly built. It refused to show even the slightest suggestions of imminent collapse, even after more than four centuries of abuse by generations of students. So much for progress in the construction industry.

This move to Magdalen College School was occasioned by my family relocating from Sheffield, a large industrial city in the north of England, to the minute Oxfordshire hamlet of Lark Rise. In order that I should not miss out on any part of Magdalen's school year, I moved south some three months ahead of the rest of the family.

During this time, I was accommodated in a delightful house occupied by an aged and saintly cleric, his wife, and his elderly sister who did nothing but refurbish her holy brother's bedsocks. As this was a continuous process, I could only conclude that he was either extremely cold or violent in bed, or that her knitting was unbelievably shoddy. This saintly cleric failed to impress Erin Forrester due, as Erin informed us, to him being 'a damned nuisance in the vestry' when assisting with school services. This condemnation only further endeared the poor man to me.

I found myself in this accommodation due to my father's calling and connections. My father, Alfred Key, was an Anglican cleric of the old school. He was a great supporter of the established church and its heritage and had finally taken up his calling relatively late in life, this after having forsaken his theological studies at the outbreak of the Second World War to join the army. This was principally to escape the clutches of an overprotective mother and his elder sister. He was eternally grateful to Herr Hitler for providing him with such an opportunity. The army pressed him into active service in rural Norfolk, where he met and married my mother and also made many lifelong friendships. Although he had a 'quiet war', he remained inordinately proud of his military career and his training as a private (the only rank that he achieved) and made much of the theoretical advantages that this conferred upon him in unarmed combat. On occasions, many decades later, when he found youths violating church property, he would bring this fact to their attention. Happily, nobody ever put these particular skills of his to the test.

Once released back into civilian life, he returned to university to complete his theological studies, eventually becoming curate of a large parish situated amongst the dark, satanic mills of Lancashire. Once he had served this brief apprenticeship, during which we lived in a tiny and crumbling terraced house, he was free to choose where to practice his ministry. He could now also fully indulge his penchant for large, impractical, tumbledown houses as a fair proportion of the Church of England's stock of vicarages and rectories qualified for this description at that time, and we certainly sampled some of the worst.

Even greater opportunity was afforded by the National Health Service, when he became a hospital chaplain in Sheffield. Of particular note was one rambling house on a site earmarked for the ultimate construction of a new hospital. This boasted extensive stabling accommodation, complete with coachman's cottage, a many roomed air-raid shelter, a butler's pantry, and an art deco ballroom, but with total absence of central heating and only rudimentary plumbing. When it was fortunately decided that this house should be demolished, before it fell down of its own accord (the substantial columns by the front door already had), we moved to a huge flat comprising part of a former nurses' home. Whilst this lacked the coachman's cottage, it did have accommodation for several horses and their carriages. An additional feature, left over from its previous occupancy was an abundant supply of toilet tissue, every sheet of which bore the worrying message, 'Government Property!' Whilst being against profligacy in the public sector, this did seem to be taking control a step too far!

When my father was offered this job, he probably became the only person of that era to consider the provision of a company car as a marked disincentive to its acceptance. He thus, reluctantly, started to learn to drive at the age of thirty-seven. Once again, Britain's military ambitions came to his help, in the form of the Suez Crisis. For some reason, it was deemed that he could learn to drive unaccompanied during this time. He thus succeeded in teaching himself to drive, fortunately without mishap.

However, his need to reverse the car into his garage each evening in order to ensure that it was ready and facing in the right direction, should an emergency arise, led to progressive and extensive remodelling of the car's rear end at the hands of the rockeries, which adorned both sides of the driveway. Always a cautious driver, for his entire life he insisted upon driving with his window fully open lest the indicators failed and he needed to make hand signals at short notice. Dressed up in overcoat and trilby hat, he was oblivious to the misery he thus inflicted on his rear seat passengers, made all the worse by his incessant pipe smoking.

Although of formidable intellect, his practical skills, upon which he depended to maintain our various homes, were not quite as well developed, as he believed. He was a capable painter and decorator, but his carpentry technique didn't stray far beyond the six-inch nail and a large hammer. When it came to electrical and mechanical skills he was positively dangerous, once managing to 'mow' the instruction book to shreds whilst, attempting to start his new motor mower for the first time. Thus, from an early age, I was warmly encouraged to learn how to execute the most basic of domestic electrical and mechanical tasks, such as fitting a plug onto an appliance. I had no difficulty in perceiving the importance of my taking on this onerous responsibility to the safety and survival of the family.

A huge bonus to my father's ambitions for our home was afforded by his hiring out of the church hall, in one of his early parishes, to an auction company. This provided him with the opportunity to purchase those lots, not sold in the auctions, for almost nothing. These items were mainly so unfashionably large as not to fit in small, modern houses, but ideal for our rambling, and initially empty, home and are now, some fifty years later, considerably appreciated in value. Less successful were the abundance of electrical items, gratefully scooped up by my mother. These usually featured frayed and disintegrating flexes at the very least. How we all survived without perishing by fire or electrocution is a wonder.

The most successful of these electrical purchases was our first television, resplendent with nine-inch screen and its huge magnifier. Unfortunately, the picture would grow darker over weeks of use, until it virtually disappeared. This was due to dust being attracted to the screen, by static, and the only solution was to remove the entire workings from their impressive mahogany cabinet and wipe the screen clean. This was one of my father's proudest achievements, which required him not only to remember to unplug the televisions from the mains, but also to reach deep into the cabinet with a large screwdriver and use it to discharge its large condenser to earth. The resulting crackle and vivid blue spark, although impressive, testified as to how potentially lethal this activity could be, if not done carefully.

Being the son of a clergyman necessitated me meeting many 'holy men,' as my mother called them. Most were charming and many eccentric, not the least of which was an Irish friend of my father's. His pronouncement on the protestant leader, Ian Paisley, was typical, 'the Reverend Ian Paisley should be strung up, no harm to him mind.' His eccentricity was acute when it came to his cars, which in deference to his calling had to be black and always required to be blessed before use. The writers of the *Book of Common Prayer* had not anticipated this eventuality, but fortunately he found, somewhere, an ancient text for the blessing of a chariot and, resplendent in full robes, would anoint his car in the street outside his house. When the need came to remember the numbers of the various keys to his car, he resorted to the hymnbook. Thus 'Oft in danger, oft in woe, onwards Christians, onwards go!' opened the doors and 'Forth in thy Name oh Lord I go!' operated the ignition. One only hoped that he accessed the correct hymnbook if he ever lost the keys. The church failed him completely when it came to a method of remembering to remove the blanket with which he cosseted the engine on frosty nights and several were hence sacrificed to the fan belt.

CHAPTER 2

LARK RISE

And so to Lark Rise, eventually, the family moved down from Sheffield and my father took over his duties as rector. The souls entrusted to my father's spiritual care numbered less than three hundred; these strung out in a series of farms and hamlets of which Lark Rise was the hub, boasting both church and school, although this had no more than twenty pupils and one schoolteacher. The nearest public house was three miles and the nearest shop also three miles away, unfortunately in opposite directions. The rectory was everything that my father could ever have wished to manifest. It was isolated, in poor decorative repair and rambling with only vestigial heating and had several acres of garden and paddocks, plus numerous outbuildings. The whole family rapidly fell in love with the place. On entering the Lark Rise rectory for the first time, we found that we had thoughtfully been left the local bus timetable by the previous incumbent; Wednesday: Banbury, Friday: Bicester.

Contrast this with the hurly-burly of the mighty city of Sheffield, which had been our home for the previous seven years, and you will appreciate what a culture shock it was. The next shock was to find a motley crew of local worthies apparently wandering at random over the rectory's extensive grounds without prior reference. They were the 'beaters' for the laird's shoot and were followed a few hours later by an even more motley local worthy bearing a brace of very dead pheasants 'for the Rector, with his Lordship's compliments.' It was fortunate indeed that my mother had been raised a farmer's daughter and was seldom happier than when up to her elbows in blood whilst eviscerating some hapless animal.

It was clear from the start that the rector needed to organise things in the village if it was to meet the challenges of the sixties. At this time, the Civil Defence organisation, successor to wartime's Home Guard, or 'Dad's Army', was still very active and became the chosen focus, largely due to my father's intense enjoyment of his brief military career. This was surprisingly popular with the local teenagers, me included, almost entirely due to the organisation's much-rumoured offer of free driving lessons for all participants. These had not materialised, however, by the time that the Lark Rise branch folded due to lack of support.

During the short life of this powerhouse of initiative, and only after signing the Official Secrets Act, we learnt vital and top-secret information to help us survive a third world war. Presumably, now, some forty odd years later it is safe to reveal at least some of the detail. In order to help us survive nuclear attack we were made privy to the innermost details of how to whitewash our windows and dig fall-out shelters in the garden. Of even greater significance was the course on nerve gasses, which were to be detected with a bicycle pump based test kit. The agreed protocol, on suspicion of a gas attack, was to pump air through the test rack for one minute, and, in the event of a positive result, don rubber facemask, and then shout 'gas'. There were only two flaws with this strategy. First of all, it was impossible to be heard whilst wearing the mask, and secondly, this was unlikely to be an issue as the gasses would have killed all within thirty miles in milliseconds. In addition, the pump fell apart when pressed into service by our instructor. Still, it all helped the passing of many a long winter evening.

As peacetime progressed, and the passing of the cold war was speculated upon, Civil Defence was one of the earliest of the paramilitary organisations to fade into the background. This left only those great paramilitary organisations inspired by Lord Baden Powell to lead the process of military indoctrination of the population—I speak, of course, of the Scouts, the Guides, the Cubs, and the Brownies.

Going back to the swinging sixties, whilst my father was mobilising the able-bodied, my mother was tending to the needs of the less fortunate, and made the sad mistake of helping one poor soul with desperately bad teeth to overcome her fear of the dentist. One evening, many weeks and many extractions after their first joint visit to the dentist, the rectory doorbell rang, and I was face to face with this good lady, tearful, but resplendent with a perfect set of teeth. She was at her wits' end, having endured a day of intense agony, trying to 'run in' her wonderful new gnashers and this after being so brave for so long.

My mother also offered help to the family who ran a small store in a neighbouring village. This store was notable for the uninspiring array of offerings in its window, their packages bleached to delicate pastel shades by stint of having been in the intermittent glare of English sunshine for many summers. It was run by Frank and his middle-aged daughter, Nancy. Whilst they earned the family's income, Frank's wife, Betty, maintained their small flat above the shop and provided a home and meals for the family, including Nancy's two brothers. Trade in the store could never have been described as brisk, and Frank, therefore, set up a second-hand television set and a couple of chairs in the storeroom where he could relax with Nancy awaiting their next customer. An ingenious system of pulleys and string connected the door of the shop to a biscuit tin full of stones, which was conveniently situated next to the television screen in such a way that should anyone enter the shop the biscuit tin would drop. Nancy and Frank, watching television in silence, would take it in strict turn to answer the bidding of the tin.

Unlike the packaging protecting the goods in his shop window, Frank's complexion had not seen the sun for many a year and, in consequence, was a ghostly white. It was thus that, after he had failed to answer the very infrequent calls of the tin for several hours, Nancy's level of frustration finally rose to such a level that she was compelled to ask her father why he was making her do all the work. After repeating this enquiry several times, each time more angry than the last, and gaining no reply, she realised something was not quite right. Frank had been dead for five hours, and the only sign of anything being amiss was his repeated failure to answer the bidding of the biscuit tin.

Nancy continued to run the store in similar vein until tragedy struck once more when Nancy's mother died. None of the family was able to cook or clean, and this is where my mother stepped in to teach Nancy the basics of housekeeping. Cleaning was as reasonable a success as my mother's failing eyesight allowed, but when it came to cooking, poor Nancy just about learnt the rudiments of hard-boiling an egg and burning toast. This was not only due to her being a poor student, but also due to her mentor's own abilities in this field, which were unusual to say the least. Nancy's brothers, who had, up to this point in their lives spent all their time fishing in the local river and watching television, were set to work in the rectory garden in the hope of teaching them something useful that might allow them to earn a living. Unfortunately, they were not good pupils and caused rather more damage to the vegetation, with their weeding, than would have been accomplished by a day's use of a heavy-duty flamethrower.

It was probably a great relief to the villagers that our next set of initiatives involved primitive attempts at animal husbandry, leaving them to go about their business much as they had done, very successfully, for centuries. Poultry keeping went largely without incident, although the ducks thoroughly enjoyed their daily swim in the overflow from the septic tank, this occurring a couple of minutes after we pulled the plug on our own ablutions.

Trouble really started with the orphan lamb, which became so used to the creature comforts of its early days when it was confined to dwelling in the warmth of the rectory kitchen that, when large enough to be banished to the paddock, it bleated non-stop whenever it observed a light on in the rectory after dark. This stiffened my father's resolve to sell it, and it departed soon afterwards, reportedly 'sent to market to find a new home.' The liberal availability of lamb chops on the rectory menu, immediately following this disappearance, suggested that this was something of a euphemistic statement.

This was followed by a piglet, purchased from the winner of the church fete's 'bowling for a pig' competition, and, despite its sex, named Flora in honour of our local bard. Unfortunately, Flora was an escapologist and would often be found indoors, having scaled the walls of his sty. This was merely a nuisance in his younger days, but two hundred pounds of pig is quite a different matter. Unfortunately, Flora was unaware of the respect that it was traditional to bestow upon a country rector, and, on rushing to assist him with some gentle gardening, by way of walking through a closed gate, was rewarded with immediate dispatch to the local bacon factory. Such was the severity of this misdemeanour, at least in my father's eyes, that no attempt was made to devise any euphemism to cover Flora's demise.

These incidents were inconsequential when compared with our final farming venture, my brother's Jersey heifer, which we acquired as a baby calf, and with which he intended to make his fortune.

All went well until Starlight reached sexual maturity and each month demonstrated the fact by forty-eight hours of incessant mooing. The solution to this was to call in the AI man from the Milk Marketing Board to inseminate her with the best-nominated bull available. This was usually to no avail, and the AI man became a very regular, albeit unusual, visitor to the rectory. Eventually, Starlight became with calf, and efforts were made to sell her, and realise her value before she gave birth. This plan would have gone without hitch had foot and mouth disease not broken out in Britain and led to a ban on all livestock movements about a month before the birth was due, and also at about the time that my brother was about to leave for the start of the university term.

My father had never been an animal lover, and any empathy he may have developed for his fellow creatures deserted him as the prospect of having a cow to milk twice a day loomed before him. One can only speculate that his particular calling stood him in good stead at this critical time, as the movement ban was lifted, and Starlight moved to her new home a matter of days before giving birth. This was only after a ceremonial visitation by the bishop to the church had been interrupted by a loud and lengthy bout of mooing. As the ceremony was about to begin, by him knocking on the church door, resplendent in cope and mitre, he paused and enquired of my father in an understanding sort of way 'Your cow, I presume?'

Cows will be a recurrent theme in this story, hardly surprising, perhaps, for someone about to embark on a career in agriculture, but the link with this fact turns out to be tenuous in the extreme.

All this occurred but a few years after the Prufumo affair, a sex scandal involving the then minister of defence and a couple of 'call girls': Kristine Keeler and Mandy Rice-Davies. In the village, there lived a very elderly, and unquestionably respectable couple, the Reverend and Mrs Needham-Davis. It was quite natural that my mother, who always had a problem with names, addressed her as Mrs Rice-Davies, and from that day onward, we all knew her as 'Mandy'. To add to Mandy's misfortunes, she insisted on acting as traffic policeman whenever her husband reversed their huge and ancient Alvis onto Lark Rise's main and only highway, which probably saw less than three cars, a tractor, and a cat pass by all day. On this occasion, preparing to make their Sunday pilgrimage to Lark Rise church, the road was clear, as usual, but she was, unfortunately, not seen by her husband who ran her over and broke both her legs, thus reducing the congregation by 20%. Happily, Mandy made a complete recovery from this mishap, and returned to swell the congregation once more.

Travel to and from Lark Rise was interesting and fraught with challenges. The bus service hardly rated a mention, as already described. As, at the start of our time here, my father was the sole qualified driver, cycling became mandatory and learning to drive became a priority for my mother and me.

The services of a local driving instructor, the unflappable Eric Swan, were engaged. Eric was possibly the most highly educated driving instructor in Britain and had left a career in teaching many years earlier, due to a nervous breakdown, and had then taken up this, apparently, to him, less stressful occupation. In times of crisis, which were many with his new pupils, he would find solace by quoting from English literature, especially Oscar Wilde. Eventually, we both passed the driving test, with no more than average driving skills, but with the added bonus of a greater appreciation of English literature.

Eric, also the partner in a local garage business, then found us a car. The car in question was a 1946 Austin 16. This aged vehicle boasted many vital accessories such as a rear window blind, sunroof, and a comprehensive built-in hydraulic jacking system, unfortunately at the expense of anything more than rudimentary braking ability. The jacking system was a constant source of family friction, as my brother would use it to lift all four wheels off the ground whilst the car was parked, causing considerable frustration to whoever next tried to drive the thing. In these early days of my driving career, I was always looking for any excuse to drive and was thus co-opted by my father to collect three aged parishioners from an outlying hamlet and deliver them to the church each Sunday evening, thereby enlarging the congregation by a very significant percentage.

My charges taught me a lot about the laws of average and variation. Although my load was only of average weight for three adults, my passengers consisted of one woman, Ms Gable, approaching twenty stones in weight, with the other couple, both of exceedingly diminutive stature redressing the balance. For some reason best known to themselves, and probably concerning their perceived safety, the three of them all sat in the back, Ms Gable, in the middle, acted as some sort of stopper with her friends wedged in on either side. Unbeknown to my passengers, on each trip I was intent upon recording a 'personal best' time for the journey. This was before the days of seat belts, the shock absorbers on the Austin were even worse than its brakes, and it was thus only a matter of time before I took a hump back bridge too fast and launched my two smaller passengers into space. Fortunately, their progress skywards was halted by the car's roof. Being grateful for the lift, they were far too polite ever to mention the incident, but were much less frequent churchgoers thenceforth.

The lack of braking ability plus the expansive nature of the bodywork, led to the Austin's demise when my mother chose to visit the convent at which she had trained as a nurse some twenty-five years previously. Being of kindly disposition, and forever grateful for having had this opportunity to work as slave labour, whilst she trained, for the princely sum of £12 per annum, she was still in awe of the place. She was therefore mortified when she managed to park the car in a hedge outside the convent whilst trying to wave a dignified farewell to the Mother Superior. The solution to this embarrassment was to replace this splendid machine with an infinitely more modest Morris Minor, much to my mother's delight, but to my distress, which was greatly compounded when I ruined the engine twice, by dint of driving at speeds that I found entirely acceptable, but that the car and my parents clearly did not.

Brackley still boasted its own railway station, and even a couple of staff to help travellers on and off the six trains per day that acknowledged Brackley as a stop. This was in the days when the concept of customer care was in its infancy, if not totally unknown. On my first attempt to travel to London, and following some altercations with the booking clerk whilst purchasing my ticket (I had failed to bring a pen to write the cheque), it seemed churlish to ask which of the two platforms was for London. It was only when I was well on my way that I discovered that I was travelling in the opposite direction; two of the day's trains departed within minutes of one another. My final experience with this travel hub was to catch the first train from the station one morning. Armed with inside knowledge that the station did not open until after this train's departure, something, which my parents found impossible to believe, I purchased my ticket the day before. Sure enough, the next morning, along with the other passengers, and in the face of a locked station, I climbed the fence, scrambled down the embankment, and boarded the train successfully.

Much of my travelling at this time was in connection with university interviews. The process of gaining a place at university was simple enough provided one had the necessary qualifications, could work out the railway timetable, and could gain the support of one's school. Given my school's obsession for getting the favoured few into Oxford, and its almost total disregard for anyone else, only the latter posed a problem. Happily, Erin Forrester, or one of his acolytes, condescended to pen the necessary recommendation to allow me to gain university entrance.

CHAPTER 3

EDUCATION

Somehow, and to my considerable delight, my schooldays were suddenly over and I bade an enthusiastic farewell to Erin Forrester and the pseudo-elite of Magdalen College School, Brackley. No more would I be forced to drive to school resplendent in the school uniform of ginger Harris Tweed jacket, and navy school cap, but my loathing of both has lasted all these years and only now, in extremis and with gently receding hairline, will I wear a hat to avoid sunburn. I have never come to terms with ginger tweed, a cross between coconut matting and extremely coarse grade sandpaper, which still serves as an all too vivid reminder of those days.

I was destined to spend the next four years, not in Erin's favoured Oxford, but in an altogether less salubrious place, albeit still on the River Thames; the town of Reading.

There is now, and was then, little to commend Reading, save the ease with which one can leave it once the mayhem of its town centre has been successfully negotiated. In those days, a day-return rail fare to London was 7/6d. (37.5p!) and, to a student, this was well worth it. Wandering around Reading, there was little of beauty, save the river Thames, and the nicest walk along the Thames first took in the gas works. Apart from the normal range of shoe shops, electrical retailers, and so forth, there were, however, some interesting specialist shops. One in particular demonstrated the versatility of marketing. In its minuscule and dusty window stood a lone rainwater gauge. For the entire four years of my sojourn in Reading, and possibly to this day, all that changed was its label which read, 'an ideal Christmas present', 'an ideal Mothers' Day present', 'an ideal Easter present' and so forth, or if seasonal inspiration failed, simply 'an ideal birthday present'. I am still unclear as to whether this marketing campaign was a complete failure, or the supply of rain gauges was infinite.

The town and the university had both benefited and suffered from its founding benefactors the local, Quaker, biscuit tycoons. It was largely as a result of them that there was a university at all, but also that, in a well-meaning, but misguided, attempt to guide the moral development of the students, the university statutes dictated much about student behaviour. These rules, amongst other things, dictated that all functions held on a Saturday finished by 11.00 p.m. in a futile attempt to ensure that all were in good shape to attend church on the Sabbath. University regulations locked the women away by 10.00 p.m. each night, with the exception of weekends when, for some unknown reason this was extended to 10.30 p.m. Any men found in the women's halls after hours, risked becoming heroes, albeit at the expense of their university education. In those enlightened days, such behaviour was rewarded with immediate termination of the offender's university career.

I was plunged into this liberal environment in October 1963, along with a couple of thousand others, mainly from single-sex schools, to continue our education in mixed-sex classes, although, of course, this all stopped by 10.00 p.m. each night. Having just left the suffocating confines of Magdalen College School and its ilk, most of us did indeed feel liberated. Nobody was watching our every move and ensuring that we completed our course work, or even attended lectures. Indeed, there were those who steadfastly avoided anything approaching intellectual effort and, instead, concentrated on having the best possible social life. There were two obstacles to this course of action: First, and most immediate, neither student grants nor, in most cases, parental generosity came close to being sufficient to sustain such a lifestyle. Second, unfortunately for them, continued access to this lifestyle depended upon passing, searching end-of-year examinations that were designed to ruthlessly cull the poorest thirty per cent of students at the end of the first year.

In the case of my chosen subject, agriculture, this culling process was encouraged by a syllabus guaranteed to discourage all but the dedicated or insane. This first year was designed to bring entrants of varying academic backgrounds up to a common level of understanding and ability in mathematics and the basic sciences of physics, chemistry, zoology, botany and, most turgid of all, geology. For me the latter three, unfortunately, became my enforced raison d'etre.

For one who had never had the opportunity to study biology at school, the practical sessions were the most frustrating. My new and impressive looking dissection kit, which included a lethal looking cut-throat razor, and many tweezers and prodders, was retired to a new life of car maintenance as soon as decency allowed and has performed sterling service in this role for many years.

The first zoology practical involved each of us meeting a very friendly looking and very recently deceased rabbit. These rabbits had been part of some bizarre nutritional study and were excessively fat, which merely served to create further impediment to our initial task of removing the entire gastrointestinal tract, measuring its components, and drawing it in detail. Inevitably, most of us were complete novices who could hardly imagine what lay beneath the seemingly impenetrable layers of fur, skin, and fat, let alone carefully dissect our way through to it. Many of us, therefore, managed to cut directly into the intestines, releasing a nauseating smell, which I can recall vividly to this day. Little did we know that we were destined to meet up with our particular rabbit's ever reducing mortal remains for many weeks as we delved ever deeper into them, the smell of freshly ruptured intestines being replaced by the all-pervading smell of the formalin in which our bunnies were preserved.

Altogether more dangerous, and infinitely less exciting, were botany practicals, which usually seemed to entail creating slivers of tissue from a lump of hardwood with the razor, which usually resulted in someone slicing the top off their finger. The relief at having survived with one's fingers intact was only tempered by the knowledge that one now had to stare down a microscope at the sliver one had succeeded in producing, identifying, and then accurately drawing its salient features. The emergency room of the nearby hospital seemed inviting by comparison.

Nothing, however, could possibly come close to the boredom of a mineralogy practical. Each Friday afternoon all that stood between us and an early start to the weekend was the task of drawing and describing twenty-five lumps of rock. An additional impediment was the lecturer who would arrive late and drone on into extra time, so it soon became imperative to start early and leave before he arrived. This poor individual's surname was 'Rose', and I always remember him fondly when I hear the song 'Rambling Rose, where you Ramble, Heaven Knows!' (and he definitely did ramble). Regrettably, he has tarnished my interest in geology forever.

My chosen accommodation was a brand new hall of residence, Windsor Hall. This masterpiece of glass, concrete, and pre-Ikea cheap Scandinavian décor was home to some two hundred to three hundred male students. One of the less successful features of the décor was the painted hessian wall-covering, much the same texture as the hated ginger tweed, but even more abrasive to the skin. A similar effect was achieved by the unbleached linen sheets, although they did at least mellow with age. Life here was, in hindsight, almost utopian. Three more than ample meals were provided, and our rooms cleaned, daily. There was a bar on site, and laundry facilities were available for those who insisted upon keeping clean. The fact that the hall was located more than a mile from the, then, main site of the university ensured that we walked several miles a day and kept reasonably fit, at least until we befriended someone with a car, something that rapidly became a priority.

Students are always hungry, a fact well known to my mother who would mail fruitcakes to me at regular intervals. These packages were always opened, in front of my expanding inner circle of friends, with some sense of speculation. Would the fruit be evenly distributed throughout the cake (unlikely), or sunken to the bottom with the surface of the cake resembling a lunar crater (a near certainty)? Also, would the cake be of normal consistency (a rarity), soggy or burnt? On the rare occasions, when the cake was close to perfection a loud cheer would go up as the first slice was tasted, but even the poorer specimens were consumed enthusiastically, a welcome and varied supplement to the standard hall fare, which featured chips at nearly every meal. Indeed, one individual insisted in keeping the score and would be heard chanting it thus 'bleedin' hell, chips again, the sixty-fifth time this term'. In an attempt to meet the students' desires, the catering manager established a suggestion book, but such is the reading ability and intelligence of the average university student that the first entry requested bathmats.

The hall was presided over by a well-meaning colonel who had recently left the relative safety of military life at the Sandhurst Military Academy to take up a sociology lectureship at Reading and to be warden of this establishment. Unwisely, he appointed as his deputy a retired naval lieutenant commander. Today, the combination of young student exuberance and retired military might would be disastrous, and it certainly struggled at that time. To start with, the warden let it be known that he wished to run the hall 'like an officer's club.' This was a mistake—especially when he attempted to ban the use of nicknames on doors, citing 'the absolute nadir of bad taste' as 'splodge.' The very next day he was faced with an epidemic of splodge door tags and disillusionment. He then attempted a fire drill—in the middle of the night. The intelligence of students is rarely in evidence, but any challenge to their sleep is likely to bring out the best, and it did. A quick look up and down the corridors and out of the windows, and no evidence of smoke, so back to bed. As a result, it took nearly half an hour to empty the building. Undaunted, he then co-opted stooges to collapse on staircases during his next attempt. These sorry individuals were lucky to escape with their lives when, after being carried down six flights of stairs in apparent agony they calmly thanked their bearers and walked away.

This duo could not last for long, and the naval presence chose to retreat. His leaving, after a particularly short and ineffective reign, taught me the important lesson that, however, difficult it may appear, it is always possible to find some positive attribute in one who is departing. In this case, it was the man's ability to find giant dustbins quickly, when the building had been commissioned without them, that formed the core of his valediction, and my only memory of him.

The routine of undergraduate university education consisted mainly of the presentation of a turgid array of facts to us students, a large and confused audience. Indeed, this was truly the presentation of false pearls before real swine, as teaching has been described. This process, as always, was highly influenced by the capabilities of the individual lecturers, many of whom were excellent, but some who were found wanting. It is perhaps inevitable, but somewhat curious, that particular subjects, often in themselves fascinating, attract particularly a charismatic individuals. Botany and geology feature high on this list and my appreciation of them was totally destroyed by the dullness of not one, but many lecturers. Economics, however, sits in a league of its own, with its substance and its advocates well matched. How a paucity of facts can be turned into a life's study and then delivered with actuarial levels of boredom is beyond human understanding.

One subject that was promoted with almost missionary zeal was statistics. The statistics department was housed in a dark eerie looking Victorian house in a wood near the centre of the campus. From this building, aptly nicknamed 'Wuthering heights', the staff would emerge to haunt the curriculum of every student, including those studying the arts, with a basic course in statistics. This was in the vain hope of improving the objectivity of the student population. Like so many missionaries, their enthusiasm for their cause was usually far greater than their ability to engender it in others. Their gargantuan task was further impaired by the primitive nature and high cost, thus scarcity, of calculating machines, which were required for the practical part of the course. Anyone who has had to share a hand-operated Facit calculating machine with an unhelpful partner, whilst carrying out complex multiplications and divisions, will understand the problem. I never truly mastered the art of using these machines, which involved turning the handle backwards and forwards, for an almost infinite number of turns, in order to execute even the most basic of calculations.

These machines and their superior electrically operated cousins were lovingly maintained by an army of mechanics who were regular visitors to any establishment dependent upon their ingenious but primitive technology. Sadly, the careers of these individuals were soon to be brought to an abrupt halt and their skills consigned to the dustbin of history along with those of door-to-door vacuum cleaner servicemen and phone sanitizers. In the former case, it was due to the development of the cheap electronic calculator, which became ubiquitous within months of its introduction. This invention should also have aided the cause of the statisticians' crusade but, sadly, there is still little evidence that decision making in business is any more objective today than was the case forty years ago; such is human nature.

The advent of the cheap electronic calculator was a boon to many who had previously relied on a shaky appreciation of mental arithmetic. These included my father in their ranks. By this stage, he had been appointed rural dean, a sort of ecclesiastical area manager, and, amongst his duties, he had to administer the expenses of the clergy under his charge. The agreed reimbursement rate for mileage incurred on church business was then seven and a half pence per mile, but my father had to increase this to eight pence in order to do the calculations. All this changed when my mother presented him with a Sinclair Cambridge calculator for his birthday, and he was then able to calculate and pay at the official rate. Hopefully, honesty prevailed among the holy recipients of these expenses, and they confessed to any reimbursement that was wildly excessive as my father would have had implicit faith in the machine and would not have noticed such error.

A valuable lesson, learned at an early stage, was not to outlive one's sell-by date. Regrettably, this rule was flaunted by several great minds of the past, which would drag themselves into the lecture theatre to transfer their wisdom, presumably by osmosis. Such wisdom included the fact that January would be a better month for making hay in Britain than June, if only the grass would grow, and, also, that a hen will quite happily lay one egg per day, provided she is fed two eggs per day.

A special place should be created for those who choose to teach and then proceed to extinguish the fires of enthusiasm. I have met many in my time, commencing with the vertically challenged and nerdy technical drawing teacher, who dismissed my first effort, when I was all of thirteen years old, with the accurate, but crushing, words of encouragement that I remember to this day, 'Well, now, this is a mess isn't it?'

This is as nothing when compared with the tardy headmaster, who, when chased to provide a reference for university entrance, asked the aspiring student why he was fretting—after all he could have been born an elephant in India, in which case university entrance would have been totally out of the question.

Alongside the routine substrate of learning, which, hopefully developed minds and identified true genius, ran our even less successful programme of social development. Happily, the drug scene was almost non-existent in this largely agricultural establishment where the wearing of jeans was considered decidedly avant-garde. The first social experimentation usually centred around alcohol, with disastrous, but usually short-lived consequences, especially for those reared under the rigours of religious fundamentalism and now suddenly free to sample the demon drink. I, for many years, held a grudge against the Welsh, as one such of their kin, having imbibed generously, would bang on my door, each evening, at midnight informing the world that '(my) da's a bloody vicar.' So much for my father's discretion in wearing his clerical collar when proudly delivering me to the hall to start my university career.

Naturally, sex was the not very holy grail of our social existence; much talked about by all, but, in those days, experienced by virtually nobody. Those who turned up at university with a steady girlfriend were the envy of all and, unfortunately, the ones we attempted to emulate. One individual is probably, to this day, unaware as to why he should have received admiring stares from so many of his hall mates. The reason for this admiration lay in the design of the building. Its boomerang shape, with his room at the centre of the concave side afforded many, fortunate enough to be housed at the building's extremities, a ringside seat to this couple's afternoon performance.

The university's calendar of social events provided a rich array of social experiences. These ranged from the weekly dances, or 'hops,' where many went in the hope of meeting a suitable partner, usually to return disillusioned, almost always due to their own ineptitude. At the other end of the spectrum were the formal dances, which were opportunities to impress one's partner with one's suavity. The problem with this was the financial outlay for formal attire. Some envied individuals possessed their own dinner jackets, but most had to hire from a seedy little tailor on the edge of town. Here one could hire the necessary outfit for a fraction of the fee demanded by the mighty Moss Bros, even if it did entail being fitted out in a large, draughty, and much windowed storeroom, where one was visible to any passers-by. A few, on particularly tight budgets, would borrow suits from their fathers, or other elderly relatives. Such suits were usually instantly identifiable by their vintage appearance and poor fit. One individual, whose aged father's dinner jacket had been in store since his own university days, had to apply boot polish to his inner thighs at each wearing in the vain hope of camouflaging the damage that many generations of moths had inflicted upon this particularly crucial area of the suit.

As the four years of the course progressed, we became more focussed on our prime objective of gaining degrees and thence employment. The university library became some sort of shrine where many spent hours, allegedly deep in study. Often they were merely staring vacantly into space as if in some form of trance, either awaiting enlightenment or atoning for their sins of omission of the previous many months. All these activities had but one goal, to somehow, whether deserved or not, achieve success in the final examinations.

The whole ritual of British university examinations at that time was perverse in the extreme. Why these should have been scheduled for May, at the height of the pollen season, when affliction with allergies could be guaranteed, and when some of the finest weather of the year could be expected, is unclear. Presumably, the additional stress and distraction was yet another test of stamina. The speed with which these balmy days disappeared and examinations materialised was truly staggering and then, immediately as the last exams were over, the heavens would open and all the plans for relaxation were thrown into touch to be replaced by an eternity of review and doubt whilst awaiting the results. In a final twist of sadism, worthy of a modern day reality show, the date when the results were to be published was always unclear and open to ill-informed conjecture. When the results were finally announced, it was in the form of lists for each class of degree, pinned on an obscure notice board. Failure was only apparent by one's absence from all the lists, leading to considerable panic as people hunted desperately for their names.

As the four years came to an end, lifelong friendships were established, degrees were granted, and engagements were announced, all within the seemingly real world in which we existed. We were blissfully unaware that the substance of all of three would be tested, in many cases to destruction, in the outside world in the years to come, or that the cracks were already showing.

CHAPTER 4

RE-EDUCATION

After one last long summer of irresponsibility, each of us armed with a piece of paper proving, at least to our own satisfaction, that we were highly intelligent, it was time to take up gainful employment. In my case, this was in the delightful, but sleepy, town of Warminster, located deep in rural Wiltshire. The first challenge was to find somewhere to live. After some enquiry, and much disappointment, I happened across an extremely comfortable looking accommodation, run by the widow of one of the town's former vicars. Using my family connections as a reference, and in spite of my appearance, I was readily accepted by the warm hearted, but outwardly severe, Mrs Belfries.

Nothing in this life is without its price, and it was inevitable that the care, comfort, and superb food offered in these digs were no exception to this rule. In this case, the price centred around the other resident, Cedric, who was deemed, by our landlady, to be of fragile constitution and who outranked me by several months' tenure. Whatever he wished in terms of radio, television, or other entertainment was to be endured by all, and I thus existed for several months on a diet of Rolls Royce refurbishment and classical music, which resonated endlessly throughout the house.

Apart from Cedric, Mrs Belfries most treasured possessions were her beloved and recently acquired beagle pup, and her Austin 1100 car. I empathise with Mrs Belfries over the subject of handwriting. Hers had caused confusion when writing to invite herself to stay with a friend, but also seeking permission to bring her new dog. She received an enthusiastic response, but containing the concerned enquiry as to why she wished to bring a bugle with her. From that day onwards, the poor dog was known as Bugle.

Unfortunately, shortly after this trip, her Austin boiled dry and the engine seized. Although she had it repaired as new, she subsequently lost faith in the car and requested that I help her replace it. Although brand new, the replacement had to be identical in every respect, so that nobody would notice her extravagance. Her honesty was such that, despite my protestations, she insisted in sabotaging my negotiation of the deal by 'coming clean' with 'the nice salesman' concerning the incident of the seized engine. Anyway, she expressed her delight with my help and rewarded me in what she believed was the most appropriate manner. It is true to say that at that stage in my life I did have difficulty in waking up in time for work, so she bought me the most fiendish alarm clock that I have ever encountered. This masterpiece of German engineering, which was probably conceived as an instrument of torture during the last unpleasantness, would start its routine with a random number of loud ticks at the appointed hour, followed by a random series of high-pitched *pings*. After this, all hell would break out as its unbelievably loud bell broke into action. Needless to say, this was the end of my tardiness; indeed, my aim was always to get out of bed during the ticking phase and silence the thing.

Another hazard was that I was expected to participate in the catching of Mrs Belfries white doves in order that they might be vaccinated. Once they had been lured into the garage, with quantities of corn, the door was slammed shut and my work began. This consisted of lunging at each and grabbing whatever came to hand. The outcome of this was half a dozen immunologically enhanced but very sorry looking tail-less fantail doves, a heap of feathers, and an unhappy landlady. It was shortly after this that I felt it prudent to leave and find a flat of my own.

The organisation to which I had offered my services was in the agricultural supply industry, a company remarkable for its technical capability and financial incompetence. In both, it was at the leading edge. When interviewed, I had visited their head office, a former country house, which still maintained some poise, despite its grounds, having been taken over by property developers to build so-called executive homes, or double-garaged rabbit hutches. Unbeknown to me, my workplace was to be at their other site, an ex army camp of World War II vintage. This site consisted of some forty odd buildings, two of which housed a couple of dozen people, the rest being home to a motley assortment of allegedly pedigree pigs who lent a characteristic and not altogether pleasant ambience to the site. Also unbeknown to me was the fact that, once again, I would be expected to sacrifice my much valued Saturday mornings to work.

After a vestigial, if not all together absent, induction programme, it was time to get down to real work and prove how little I really knew. This was all the more urgent as it soon became apparent, even to its financial director, that the company was in a very serious plight indeed. Step one of the board's recovery plan, as is so often the case, was to rename the company, adding the tag 'International' and then to repaint every vehicle, irrespective of age, condition or mobility, in a new and expensively designed livery; a sign of impending corporate death, which I now recognise instantly. In addition, to emphasise the company's global ambition, it opened an office in Brussels and, as none of the export team wanted to live in such distant and foreign territory, employed a new and completely unknown staff to run it, subsequently expressing complete surprise when their monthly expenses rivalled the national debt. Step two was to close the head office and for the corporate overhead, to join the pigs and the technical team at the ex army camp. Opportunity was taken at this time to attempt removal of the aged one-time managing director, who, at the time of an earlier reorganisation, had agreed to step down, but only if paid the then considerable salary of £4,000 per annum for life and if allowed to haunt the marketing department forever. No office was allocated to this ageing tyrant, but a sick room was established, only to be hijacked by him. He immediately glued his name to the door in six-inch high letters. Thus ensconced, he then continued to terrorise anyone who crossed his path, especially if young, female, and attractive. Fortunately, I only qualified for mild chastisement, this on the basis of the first of these criteria.

I found myself reporting, not to the charming head of research who had led the interview process, but to his right hand man, Derek Thrapp. Derek was talented, wonderfully eccentric, and absolutely maddening as one's boss. He worked his own form of flexitime, long before this had been invented. Unfortunately, his working day tended to start as everyone else was going home, this largely to accommodate every whim of his domineering wife who made sure that he undertook at least his full share of the care of their children. He totally failed to understand why others did not wish to while away their evenings discussing business, which should have been dealt with hours previously. Possibly, in a futile effort to encourage him towards more reasonable behaviour, he was required to clock in and out every day. He complied enthusiastically, feeding his punch card into the time clock each of the many times he passed it every day. Derek could be relied upon to find a novel solution to any problem, whether related to his business or personal life.

Whilst the former justifiably accounted for his success within the company, the latter led to some interesting situations. For example, his secretary would often find her office occupied with one or more of his children, expected to combine their care with her regular duties, when they were unable to go to school due to sickness. Derek also enjoyed a glass of wine with his dinner and would expect business guests to find their own way to his favourite restaurant whilst himself cycling the several miles to it from his home, thus avoiding any possible risk of being caught driving under the influence.

Derek struggled with the concept of inherited wealth and position, something of a problem given the ownership of the company that employed him. He confessed himself to be strongly in favour of a meritocracy, although I suspect that his definition of merit involved the possession of a degree in zoology from one of the less well-known British universities and a diploma in tropical agriculture comfortably achieved at the University of the West Indies, the very qualifications, which he possessed. As an aside, the latter course was subsequently transferred to a British university of greater academic excellence much to the chagrin of its potential students who could no longer expect to enjoy tropical bliss in exchange for a gentle expenditure of mental effort. Timeliness featured nowhere in Derek's personal rating of merit, and it was commonplace to be kept waiting hours for a prescheduled appointment.

It was at this time that I first met Angus McPhee, who was then the company's production manager. Whilst his seniors were busy frittering away money on their rescue plan, he exercised his Scottish lack of generosity to full effect in spending as little of the company's money as possible, whilst just about managing to keep the wheels of the business turning. He applied similar control to the dissemination of information from his department. His subordinates had presumably signed something more intimidating than the Official Secrets Act, judging from their unswerving obedience to his every wish, which included putting in an appearance on Saturday mornings, his department turning out to be the only one where this was arcane practice was observed to any significant extent.

The company possessed but two serious electrical calculating machines, and these were heavily utilised by the research department and by Angus who was constantly developing complex financial models of plans to shave ever-smaller amounts off the production budget. Competition for these machines was intense, especially as, once Angus got his hands on the most sophisticated machine, his favourite, it would sit on his desk, largely unused, for days whilst he responded to the constant call of his telephone. Even when going out, he would lock the machine in his office, so that it would be instantly available to him upon his return, whenever that might be. So irritating did this behaviour become that one of the research staff, happily another Scot who could talk to him in language that he would instantly understand, decided to request that Angus should consider the needs of others. Predictably, Angus declined to modify his behaviour and so irritated his challenger that he swept all of Angus's mountainous paperwork off his desk and onto the floor. Angus smiled weakly to an onlooker, remarking that his assailant would be back shortly to apologise. This has yet to happen.

Despite this shortage of calculators, the company did possess a computer. In a seemingly far-sighted move, and to support their research department, they had bought one of the very last ICT 1202 machines for what seemed like a bargain price. Unfortunately, this move was about as logical as it would have been to purchase a steam locomotive in the advent of the diesel. Like a steam locomotive, it was impressive and noisy, being about the size of a house, filling the building with interesting sounding clatter, and possessing several wardrobe-sized compartments full of glowing valves. It provided sterling service, but, by the time I arrived, programming the thing was difficult as its programming language was by now ancient history, besides which mice were now resident in its depths, attracted by its warmth, causing urgent and frequent need for maintenance whenever they chewed into any particularly important wire.

Spurred on by the prospect of forthcoming decimalisation, management was encouraged to replace this behemoth with a sleek looking ICL 1900 series computer, lured by the prospect of being able to attract external customers for its services. For some reason, computer salesmen thought that computing needs would be far greater when British business was faced with the daunting prospect of having to divide everything by ten, rather than a mix of twelve and twenty. Suffice it to say that no external clients ever materialised. The situation was further compounded by the thing having to live in a purpose built air-conditioned palace and be lovingly tended by a small army of highly paid and temperamental operatives.

I gradually began to feel at home in my work environment. In part, this came out of the camaraderie of adversity. As the company's performance worsened and many employees were made redundant, those of us remaining grew closer together. A major feature of each day became our communal sandwich lunch where we reviewed the latest corporate rumours and swapped weak jokes. Most of us brought a small package of food, but Tom, chief pig technician, and as lean as a rake, brought a duffle bag brim full of food. A staple of Tom's diet was beetroot sandwiches, which made him appear unattractively Dracula-like, when laughing in mid chew as the beetroot juice dripped through his teeth. Tom was one of the most miserly individuals I have ever met, never having any spare cash on him and even selling his surplus garden produce. He even managed it such that his daughter's birthday was 29 February. To his credit, he now has the most beautiful home, this being the direct result of decades of parsimony.

While I was getting into my career, two significant events took place in my personal life: The first of these was to become a homeowner at a time when the building societies believed that they were doing anyone an enormous favour to lend money to buy a house, the sole purpose for which they had been established. It was thus that my attempt to obtain a mortgage was dismissed as theft by the uninspiring streak of humanity who filled the role of chief clerk at my chosen lender, 'now you really can't expect to come in here and steal three thousand pounds, having only been with us six months and having amassed a mere one hundred pounds in your account. Go away and save one thousand pounds, and then we'll talk.' Clearly, on a salary of one thousand pounds, this was going to take some time. However, somehow, the necessary loan was obtained from another source and house ownership became a reality. This was one of those occasions when Erin Forrester's immortal words, 'Banks will take anything as long as it moves and breathes,' provided me with some comfort.

The other milestone, following on from the inevitable university engagement, was marriage. Suffice it to say that, the longer I live the more confidence I have in the science of genetics.

Perhaps longer spent getting to know my prospective mother-in-law would have saved a lot of anguish.

In the late 1960s, corporate life was dominated by takeovers, and the business pages of the daily papers were full of praise for the asset strippers. It was inevitable that such corporate shambles should attract the attentions of one of the lesser players in this game and, in a period of a month, the company was bought and sold twice. The speed with which the asset strippers moved was only rivalled by the extent of their exaggerated claims. They arrived on the first morning of their ownership to address the management. This group of 'experts' in our business promised vast investment in the company. Just where these experts had been hiding, why we had never heard of their spectacular careers before, and why they should be about to invest millions in such a poor business should have been of concern to all. Whether Derek Thrapp had realised this and chosen to boycott the meeting, or, whether his arrival in its closing moments was just due to his usual tardiness, or another family crisis, is unclear, but he certainly avoided the waste of a perfectly good morning. As we should have predicted, the company, having been relieved of a few pieces of prime development land, was immediately sold on. It thus ended up in safer, but only marginally more capable hands. The outcome of this was the absorbing of the company by its new owners, and the final surrender of my office to the pigs.

I was offered, and accepted, a transfer to a position in Carlisle, and set forth on this new adventure within one of Britain's largest companies, only to find myself working in a converted cowshed. This time the cows had completely vacated the site, but few other changes had been made to these dark, unheated, stone-floored facilities.

This work environment was luxurious in comparison to the accommodation that greeted me upon my arrival. I was driven to a dinghy suburb of Carlisle, a city so close to the north west border of England and Scotland that it was unsure whether it was in either or neither of these countries, but which, just to be on the safe side, tended to celebrate the holidays of both. I was ushered to the dull front door of an anonymously ugly terraced house and rang the bell. The reply was instant; the remote (but rapidly growing nearer) barking of multiple hungry sounding dogs, the opening of the front door to be filled by a large woman, perspiring freely, and the stench of much boiled cabbage. As I looked past this apparition, I was aware of the hallway, a dirty brown cavern. 'Are you the shift worker?' the woman screeched, before leading me upstairs to my prospective new home, another dirty brown cell which, I suspected would have been my home time—about with some other unfortunate who worked nights and could thus utilise my bed during the day. The look of horror on my face must have registered, because I was immediately checked into an hotel pending the finding of something more acceptable.

Soon I was more or less happily ensconced in perfectly comfortable accommodation, pending my purchase of a new home, and I settled down to my daily toil in the converted cowshed.

This change of job also served as my introduction to exotic travel, albeit only to Yorkshire a hundred miles away. Fortunately, for me, I had already served time in this county whose sons believe it to rank rather higher in God's universe than it warrants as a mere county of England. Unfortunately, for me, my prime contact in Yorkshire displayed an excess of this credo. He combined this with the ability to be completely ineffective and display gross short-sightedness and an overdeveloped love of pigs.

Alf, or 'Piggy Dick,' as he was known was a wonderful man with whom to occupy drinking time, when he would spend many happy hours waxing lyrical on the mating activities of pigs, in one of the many quaint Yorkshire taverns, which thrived on his patronage. Unfortunately, he was a total disaster when it came to business. Alf was not totally devoid of skill, however, particularly when faced with me querying whether any action had occurred, since my last visit, on the ever growing list of issues which he had promised to progress. His tactic was to pick up his car keys and fiddle with them gently for a few minutes, and then to suddenly hurl them skywards and attempt to catch them, a feat at which he would only succeed very occasionally due to his extreme short-sightedness and general incompetence. The unpredictability of this action always succeeded in diverting my train of thought and thus ending my line of enquiry. It also usually resulted in me setting off on the long journey home in despair as to the futility of the task. If I was particularly unlucky, this would be only after a car journey with him, which was always fraught with excitement due to his lack of sight and attentiveness to the task in hand, often heightened by his partiality to alcohol.

In between my weekly forays across the country to visit Alf, I would endeavour to encourage progress by phoning him most days. I always commenced my calls by enquiring as to how he was. Alf had only two answers to this enquiry, an overenthusiastic, 'Wonderful dear boy,' or the one I dreaded, a suicidal sounding, 'Miserable.' If this was his response, it would take much gentle counselling to elicit any other words from him and, indeed, when first faced with this response I feared that he was now lying comatose, or worse at the other end of the phone. The underlying cause of his mood was always the performance of his favourite boars at the artificial insemination centre that he ran. If these unfortunate creatures had succumbed to Alf's porcine advances and, at the critical moment, transferred their affections to the thoughtfully provided artificial sow, all was bliss. Any other outcome turned Alf into abject misery personified. Happily, I was usually spared the intimate details of these trysts.

My time in Carlisle was destined to be a mercifully short eighteen months. Rationalisation within the company led to closure of the Carlisle offices, which were acquired by a property developer and transformed into an attractive residential complex, all evidence of their previous bovine associations being successfully erased by the developers.

CHAPTER 5

OVER THE BORDER

I now found myself, much against my desires at the time, moving to Scotland. The whole experience of my introduction to Scotland in the early seventies could be summarised in one word 'bleak.' As one approached its capital, Edinburgh, the parapets of one of the railway bridges were daubed with the message 'English go home,' which I felt to be directed towards me, personally. What a greeting as one planned my relocation to Scotland, and whatever traumatic experiences emboldened someone sufficiently for them to risk life and limb scaling this bridge to leave this crude message?

Moving there in midwinter, the weather was cold and wet with daylight virtually non-existent.

Emphasising this bleakness is the huge amount of stone used in buildings and subsequently blackened by the Industrial Revolution. To complement this, allegedly due to lack of local availability of good quality brick, the vast majority of houses built in the last century are covered by a cheap looking off-white stucco, which rapidly becomes a dismal shade of grime. It isn't by chance that Dunfermline became known as the 'Auld Grey Toon,' and this certainly appeared to be an understatement on that all too typical dull, wet November day of my first encounter. Like Scotland itself, even Dunfermline redeemed itself in my eyes over the years, as I became familiar with it, despite its dreariness.

The first task was to buy somewhere to live. In Scotland, unlike most places in the world, the advertised asking price for a house is usually set somewhere below the lowest aspiration of the vendor in a particularly melancholy moment, whereas his expectation is always far greater than one can possibly afford. Sealed bids, which are binding, are submitted to the seller's solicitor by a closing date. This system, designed to extract a healthy, and wholly undeserved, stream of fees for the various professionals such as surveyors, lawyers, and lending agencies, who have to be consulted in advance, is daunting to deal with for the first time. It also ensures the highest possible price for the vendor as desperate buyers attempt to offer sufficient to guarantee their success and avoid them repeating the whole expensive cycle again and again. Over the years, the system has become more sympathetic to the buyer, but at that time, it certainly threatened to totally deplete my meagre financial resources.

On buying my house, I discovered that I had purchased a 'feudal dwelling.' As this was a modern house, I was somewhat surprised at this description, until I discovered that this referred to the fact that I now had a feudal laird, the local Earl. He lived in a once impressive, but now distinctly faded residence, which his forbears had thoughtfully built on a cliff above the village, situated such that the homes of his serfs did not interfere with his magnificent view of the Firth of Forth beyond. In recognition of him having once owned and sold the land on which my house was situated for a vast sum, he had certain rights, for example to determine what colour I could paint my front door. In view of the fact that this individual cared little for any of the village that he couldn't actually see from his stately pile, and was steadily selling off as much of his farmland as he could for sprawling development, this seemed an unnecessary privilege for him to be afforded. I was at least relieved to learn that he no longer had the right to charge me feudal duties. These annual fees had previously been due from feudal 'tenants' to their laird, again in recognition of him having deigned to sell off his land to the lower classes.

What makes Scotland more than the scenery (when one can actually see it) is the warmth and welcoming nature of its people. Although the weather and especially the winters can be drear, the Scots make up for it by their excess of partying. Although Christmas is, nowadays, celebrated at least as enthusiastically as is the case in England, it is but a warm up for New Year's Eve, or Hogmanay, as the Scots know it. Regrettably, as with all Scottish occasions, Scotch whisky is central to this celebration. This particular form of alcohol with its unpleasant taste to any first timer is definitely not worthy of further familiarisation as I certainly learnt to my cost on my first Scottish Hogmanay. In the cold light of day, the practice of staying home until midnight and then spending a freezing cold winter's night visiting as many of one's neighbours as possible in order to toast their good health for the New Year with both your whisky and theirs can instantly be seen to be as insane, as it actually is. Suffice it to say that my first experience of this, and the ensuing hangover, has cured me of drinking whisky forever. After a brief respite, the Scots then celebrate their national poet, Rabbie Burns, with another alcoholic extravaganza, the Burns supper, on 25 January. This time the whisky is accompanied by haggis, the national dish of sheep offal and oats boiled in a sheep's stomach (detached from its donor). This, surprisingly, is quite delicious. Apart from the eating and drinking, this celebration is legitimised by the cultural exploit of recitation of Burns's poetry and songs and toasts to his memory. Regrettably, it takes several years experience of the Scots dialect to even begin to understand most of this wonderful poetry, but this matter less and less as the evening progresses.

As soon as I came to terms with the fact that Scotland was indeed a different country, with its own rich culture, rather than being a bit of England that happened to be a long way from London and was usually characterised by appalling weather, I grew to love the place. This was so much the case that, unknown to me at the beginning, I was destined to live there for the next thirty years.

To round off the initial experience of bleakness, my new office, although never inhabited by pigs or cattle, was dull and uninspiring. An austere and rather clinical element was created by the telephonist/receptionist who greeted one, resplendent in surgical gloves, rather as if she was about to perform some sort of intimate surgical procedure. The reason for this was somewhat more mundane; the ancient plug-board telephone exchange was prone to giving its operator regular electric shocks. Rather than replace it, the rather acerbic managing director of the time, whose voice alone may have been responsible for the unusually high voltage passing through this device, came up with the cost saving solution of a pair of rubber gloves to insulate the operator from the plug board. It was gratifying, however, that the phones were sanitised by the Phonotas lady every week. This practice was stopped after a few years with absolutely no perceptible impact on the level of ear infections within the office.

Things were looking up on the work front, and I now merited, joy of joys, a company car. At this time, Ford of Britain was riding high with its product range, which was pitched to tickle the egos of aspiring executives. It did this by supplying its Cortina with a wide range of engines and trim packages, which allowed companies to pigeonhole their executives on the executive ladder by the car with which they were allocated. This managed to divert the mental processes of these same executives from realising that the car, in all its forms, was an appallingly built heap of crap. The fact that so many wasted so much time worrying about exactly which of the myriad of models would be theirs, and how this would impress their friends, explains a lot about the decline of British industry. At this stage, I was only too delighted to get anything, but this delight began to fade as I realised the performance limitations of my particular barge with its miniscule engine and lack of features. Indeed the thing was a death trap, fortunately painted luminous yellow so that people could take avoiding action when they saw it approaching. The colour choice for these vehicles was alarming, with luminous blue, yellow, and green as prominent options, but camouflaged by innocent sounding names. It was thus that one ageing executive found himself driving, and justifying his choice of, a luminous green vehicle (very safe). Admittedly, he had mistakenly expected the colour afforded the title of 'Le Mans Green' to be British Racing Green, but neither should have materialised as luminescent.

The justification for my vehicle was largely occasioned by my continued need to constantly visit the company's operations in Yorkshire, which were now a lengthy two hundred miles from my office. Although I more than redoubled my efforts to help Piggy Dick improve the workings of his operation, the task was more than a match for my interpersonal skills, and those of many others, and poor Alf was 'moved sideways' to a position where his chaotic management style could wreak less havoc, whilst not separating him from his beloved pigs. He did somehow survive within the organisation until retirement age, which was no mean feat in itself, given his general level of incompetence.

Piggy Dick ultimately met his end after a very few years of retirement. Tragically, he engaged the services of a tree surgeon to fell a tree in his garden. He then ventured out to enquire about progress at the least opportune moment and the tree fell directly upon him, thus concluding a lifetime crowded with misadventure.

After a few years of successfully liaising with Yorkshire, my first chance to engage in serious overseas travel arose, and I set forth on a month's visit to New Zealand.

CHAPTER 6

THE ANTIPODES

It was with great naivety and some excitement that I set forth in October 1983 for a different continent for the very first time in my life. Such was the generosity of my employer that I was dispatched steerage class on this longest possible journey from Heathrow Airport. As I boarded the plane, various concerns occupied my mind—would I get dinner on board? Was a pair of headphones to listen to the in-flight movie a justifiable business expense? Did the captain know the way?

By the time, we arrived at our first stop, Bombay, the initial excitement had long gone to be replaced by acute boredom. Bombay airport did little to blunt this, with its dirty brown and cream décor, reminiscent of a British railway station circa 1950. On re-boarding the plane, I met my new travelling companions; two members of a Russian cycling team, on their way to Auckland, complete with spare wheels. For the next eighteen hours, I was hemmed in at the window by the two of them and, with no common language, conversation was impossible, although about halfway through, one of them offered me a custard cream biscuit, a genuine and much appreciated attempt at the entente cordiale.

Later, I learned that their travel on British Airways was due to the refusal of all other airlines to carry the team in protest to the recent shooting down of a Korean Airlines 747, which had inadvertently strayed into Russian airspace. Quite why British Airways should have afforded them this courtesy, I have no idea; it seemed a strange occurrence in Thatcher's Britain. It is sad to record that the cycling team's journey was of little avail; the poor quality of their Russian made tyres was no match for the punishing New Zealand terrain, and they had to return home dejected and without honour.

Eventually, after the longest twenty-six hours that I had ever experienced, and without managing a wink of sleep, I landed at Auckland airport. Even in my confused and comatose state, I was aware that I was at the end of the earth. Both New Zealand and New Zealanders emanate an aura of the faraway. This is exemplified by their lifestyle of wanderlust. The world is full of New Zealanders, wandering around trying to find the things that they fear they might have missed out on by living in New Zealand. Although the population of the country was then only three million (plus sixty million sheep), I believe that it would have been two or three times this if they had been content to just stay in their own country (like the sheep).

I admit to arriving in New Zealand with less than an open mind concerning the country and its occupants. This stemmed from an event some years earlier where as a very junior member of my company's management team I was summoned to the managing director's office, along with many of my seniors, to be addressed by the head of our New Zealand subsidiary. We were treated to a poor and lengthy discourse on the operation, which not only indicated how pathetically small in scale the business actually was, but also described every building on their tiny farm and its occupants in mind-numbing detail. This was subsequently followed by an appalling amateur video, memorable both for its poor quality and by virtue of its demonstration of the lack of proficiency of the local management. This experience has been etched on my memory forever and has prejudiced me against both New Zealanders and amateur video.

I was picked up at the airport and shown the sights of Auckland before being taken to my motel to sleep for a few much-needed hours before dinner. Unfortunately, my sleep began prematurely, and I missed out on the sights—or so I thought, until many years later when I revisited the city, only to realise that despite its idyllic harbour location, it was but an unbelievably pale imitation of Australia's Sydney Harbour. The paucity of imagination, which led to this, was evident in all too many aspects of New Zealand life, and nowhere more than in its motel accommodation. New Zealand motels are usually insipid in décor and, in my experience, all rooms contain the statutory domestic refrigerator complete with a bottle of milk in honour of the country's staple industry. Add the kettle jug and, on waking up jet lagged and disorientated, one is in no doubt as to one's location. Switch on the television and confirmation is instant in the form of news reports on calf-rearing and sheep-shearing competitions interspersed with a menu of other sports and aged instalments of British and American soap operas. It would be interesting to know how many businessmen have not only contemplated suicide at this wakening, but also actually succumbed to the temptation.

After an overnight stop in Auckland, I travelled to New Plymouth, a little town in the shadow of Mount Taranaki, an extinct volcano, featured on every postcard of the area, due to its picturesque, snowcapped appearance. If Auckland was uninspiring, this took such description to a new low. On arrival, I checked into the local motel, only differing from the New Zealand norm by its purple décor. This extended to every feature of the building and three weeks of it certainly constituted overdose. During these three weeks, I was to see the mountain as featured in the picture postcards only once, and then only briefly, due to the allegedly atypically wet weather. I remain unconvinced of this atypicality, mainly on account of the liberal availability of umbrellas and umbrella racks in all public places.

New Zealand in the early 1980s was at least twenty-five years out of date by Western standards. Whilst seldom open for business on weekdays, it was definitely closed at weekends when sport, drinking, the nursing of major hangovers (which naturally extended to Mondays and, in more than a few cases, to the whole week) and sleeping were the usual pastimes. After three days in this place, I was asked if I would like to live in New Zealand. Unfortunately, I answered with total honesty, that I would not, only to be asked why this was the case. Here, honesty failed me; after all, I could hardly describe how boring I had found the country to be. I did, however, manage to describe its major attribute as 'being very green.' In fairness, it has to be said that the countryside, even in the North Island is beautiful, and I was yet to visit the South Island, which by all reports was spectacular. Nevertheless, I find the bland architecture and lack of obvious history unappealing.

Nowhere embraces the concept that anyone who arrives from overseas on a big silver bird must be an expert more than New Zealand, and I know many who manage a very comfortable existence thanks to this phenomenon. As a novice to overseas travel and work, I was extremely grateful for the protection afforded to me by this umbrella. The company that I was visiting was small, but I was amazed by their ability to provide me with a new audience every day to listen to my words of supposed wisdom. I suspect that even the cleaners were forced to attend. I was also thankful that the questions posed by these audiences were exceedingly mundane and easy to answer, although after several days it all became rather tedious.

After I had given talks to what seemed to me to be approaching the entire population of New Zealand, the practical part of my work began, and for over two weeks, I was expected to shower in and out of their facilities. The showering ritual is usually practiced most ardently where hygiene and management routines are the most suspect, and this was no exception. Supervisory staff had excused themselves from showering as they were 'too busy,' and clearly too important to harbour disease organisms. My lasting memory of this ritual is the smell of the mandatory shampoo that of cheap synthetic honeysuckle fragrance; undoubtedly, the result of an unfortunate bulk purchase—no wonder that it was a good buy. Its noxious perfume stuck to one, like glue, for hours. One of the shower units was just over three times the size of the others in all dimensions except height. The plans had been drawn in feet but executed in metres. Presumably, as the building rose in stature, it dawned on the management that the building was intended for people rather than giraffes and common sense prevailed. A cursory review of the plans prior to construction would have saved a lot of cost and angst, but such a precaution appeared to have escaped the minds of those concerned. This issue of confusing imperial and metric units is not unique and even had caused problems with America's space programme. On balance, I am rather relieved that the New Zealanders confined their efforts to bathrooms rather than shooting for the moon.

Into this bleak landscape came a hefty glimmer of hope in the form of Bernard Peacock. Bernard, an Englishman, who had forsaken his native land some thirty years previously, in retirement, had discovered the reason for existence, not in his adopted country but in Thailand. This very largely centred on him believing that he had found true love in this exotic location. This was no mean feat for a pensioner, whose teeth would have kept the team at the local dental hospital fully committed for several months had they attempted the task of restoring Bernard's rotting fangs. The other impediment to true love was Bernard's wife, Mrs P, who was considerably less charismatic than Bernard and who lavished the bulk of her attentions on their Siamese cat, Noisette or Nausette, as Mrs P unfortunately insisted on pronouncing it. The fact that this poor creature was also male served to further confuse its identity.

Mrs P had the patience of a saint and could sit in the couple's ancient (circa 1965), and gently dented, Ford Falcon for hours. She had had much practice at this as Bernard was wont to allow her to accompany him on short domestic business trips and then forget that she was with him until his interest in the project at hand waned many hours later, when he usually returned to his car, only to find her sitting exactly where he had left her. On rare occasions, she had inadvertently left the vehicle for a few moments, sometimes to find it missing on her return. The problem was that, in these cases, Bernard was blissfully unaware of the empty seat beside him, possibly until home and waiting for the next meal to be presented. Missing a journey with Bernard was, however, on balance, a considerable blessing. On the open road, he would drive by feel rather than sight and when manoeuvring, caused grievous and frequent harm with his tow bar. These habits had absolutely no effect on his car whose multiple scars merely added to its character.

Bernard, who had led a distinctly average life during his long business career, shone during his supposed retirement. Apart from his frequent rejuvenating forays into Thailand, he was the CEO's confidant and special projects manager. As such, he had free reign to wreak revenge on those who had thwarted him prior to his retirement and to research the company's archives to provide the necessary evidence. Added to this the wisdom of years, and a not inconsiderable intellect, and he was a force with which to be reckoned.

Life for New Zealanders at that time was difficult enough without such threats. After generations of exploitation of the indigenous population, the Maoris, whose culture (where not destroyed by the incomers) left the only vestiges of history that the country possessed, they had become aware of racism. It was thus that everyone was desperately keen to be able to testify to a modest and known inclusion of Maori blood, and they certainly attempted to emulate the Maoris in their excessive consumption of beer and cigarettes, usually with considerable success. This sudden awareness of their Maori heritage, however, did nothing to push their own culture beyond sports or their appreciation of architecture beyond the uninspiring ticky-tacky boxes in which they lived.

My hosts were extremely generous and determined to show me their country. At the end of three weeks, I believed that I had fully exhausted all the work and sightseeing opportunities that the North Island offered and was desperate to return home, but this was not allowed until they were convinced that I had seen every conceivable landmark that they could conjure up.

Only New Zealand could feature sheep and kiwis as major tourist attractions. Surrounded on every side by the things, they created the sheep-a-rama where all manner of breeds of sheep were displayed on stage or actually sheared before a bewildered audience. The kiwi, being the national bird, was proudly displayed, but unfortunately, being nocturnal, one had to creep into a poorly lit tunnel to catch it unawares. Needless to say, it managed to hide with total success on the occasion of my visit.

During my time in New Zealand, I visited the hot springs at Rotorua. Had these been man-made, they would have been closed down as both a safety and an environmental hazard. The spectre of many sulphurous pools bubbling away, with geysers spraying forth weakly did not match my expectations. The cause of this may have been the New Zealanders themselves who, faced with a free energy source, tapped it over liberally to heat their homes, thus weakening the wonders of the geyser display. The kiwi fruit is a similar New Zealand success story. With considerable ingenuity, their plant geneticists exploited this interesting fruit that soon gained acclaim in many parts of the world and led to a sizeable trade in the export of kiwi fruit. New Zealand then exported vines to all and sundry, leaving the local market at disadvantage due to its remoteness from the rest of civilisation. In Harold Macmillain's words, they had 'sold the family silver.'

My final act upon leaving New Zealand was to purchase souvenirs for my children at Auckland Airport. It is comforting to note that, over twenty years later, my daughter was able to report that the self same pictorial twelve-inch ruler that I had purchased for her in 1983 was still available at the airport shop. Such is progress in New Zealand.

On returning home, I was seeking enlightenment as to whether my view of New Zealand was unfair. Travelling home in my car one evening, I heard what I thought was a religious talk in which an individual had asked a fellow traveller if he knew the meaning of death. Awaiting a pearl of life-changing information, he was provided with the reply, 'life in New Plymouth'. I may have been the only listener who truly appreciated that reply. Some years later, still (despite two further visits) worried at my attitude to the place, I asked a Japanese acquaintance, who had spent several years of his life in Australia, for his view on New Zealand, 'Mr Key,' he replied politely, 'I think they aspire to be Ghost Town.' My mind was finally at rest.

Chapter 7

Into Africa

Having circumnavigated the globe merely to visit New Zealand, I was now a seasoned traveller and ready for more serious assignments.

South Africa, in 1984, was still ruled by the Nationalist Party who, with the aid of the heavy grip of apartheid, ensured that it was a wonderful place for the privileged white minority to live. This too was the superficial view that greeted the visitor when he arrived in Johannesburg; at least once, he had negotiated the unpleasant rigours of immigration.

It is increasingly my experience that the essence of a nation's character is found in its purest form in its immigration staff, be it the bureaucratic, but disinterested staff at Heathrow or the now friendly post-apartheid multiracial clerks that greet you in South Africa. Jan Smuts (now Johannesburg International) Airport in these earlier days was a different story. One left the brilliant sunshine of the South African dawn to enter the grim grey formality of the immigration hall. After queuing in the slow moving lines, one could guarantee to be greeted by a vision of Afrikaner unfriendliness, who would examine the totally irrelevant, and lengthy, immigration form line-by-line before laboriously attaching his stamp and motioning you into his beloved country, a more unpleasant experience than entering many communist states at that time. This grim bureaucracy was typical of the country, as was the immigration form that asked each of its irrelevant questions twice—on one side of the form in Afrikaans, and on the other in English. Imagine the horror of being awoken into the very early African dawn, and immediately trying to complete the Afrikaans side of the form left for you by the cabin attendant, unaware that the other side was printed in a language that you could actually understand. Quite why the Afrikaans language, a corruption of Dutch, itself a minority language, should be sustained is unclear. It is spoken by only five million whites, who all understand English and who generally, refuse to learn the indigenous African languages. Its harsh guttural sound can hardly have encouraged its preservation as a vehicle for poetry and prose.

Needless to say the process of entering and leaving New Zealand has left no permanent impression on my memory, save their annoying practice of charging a leaving fee of twenty New Zealand dollars, to be paid in local currency, which has caused much frustration to many who have emptied their pockets of the wretched stuff before departing for the airport.

This first visit to South Africa occurred in June in the depth of winter. On the Transvaal, this is a season of no rainfall, and all the vegetation becomes tinder dry and brown. The daylight hours are blessed by warm, brilliant sunshine, but the cool evenings and sub-zero night-time temperatures provide many challenges. This is especially true for the natives, who attempt to keep warm in the early mornings by donning tartan travelling rugs and creating a roadside glow by setting fire to the vegetation. The first of these habits is merely strange—why the tartan travelling rugs? Did some wily Scot make his fortune thus? The second is more serious often leading to uncontrollable fires that wreak havoc for miles.

I was taken from the airport to the place that was to become my home-from-home over the next few years. Meyerton is a nondescript Transvaal town some thirty miles south of Johannesburg. Situated in a poor farming area, infiltrated by heavy industry, its Afrikaner population, even by the standards of those days was far from the leading edge of liberalism. It boasted one hotel, 'the Meyerton Hotel,' conveniently situated by the railway sidings where trains clanked and jostled through the small hours of the night. This hotel was probably very similar to hundreds in small industrial Transvaal towns and was universally drab. The management certainly saw no need to invest in paintings, or anything else, which might make it more attractive. The hotel had an off-licence, which served as a conduit to transfer the limited financial resources of the black population to the hotelier's pockets and a public bar, which served a similar purpose for the less affluent whites of the district. It also boasted a ladies' bar, not for the exclusive use of the fairer sex, but rather for men to use when they could not avoid being accompanied by their wives. Fortunately, it was this bar that served the restaurant and thus allowed one to go to dinner without having opportunity to partake in the fights that were a nightly occurrence in the public bar.

Two affable black waiters, Lucas and Nelson, served in the restaurant, resplendent in white shirts, black bow ties and elderly yellow jackets. Lucas served with an attempt at suavity that was clearly the result of having watched far too many second-rate American movies. The well-meaning Nelson could never have been termed suave, even without the heavy Biro stains on the top pocket of his yellow jacket, which lasted the full five years of my many visits. The food that they served up was basic, but good, largely consisting of steaks for which South Africa ranks high in the world league of quality. On Sunday evenings, the à la carte menu was not available and, after a guessing game with Nelson that filled several Sunday evenings, it became apparent that his 'table d'hôte' menu consisted of but one dish, a cheese omelette. Even with this one dish, an extensive choice of wonderful South African wines was on offer, which helped to make up for any disappointment concerning the food choice.

My room, Room 2, was dinghy, another incarnation of the brown and cream décor that I hate so much. It was sparsely furnished with bed, wardrobe, desk, and an upright chair and totally lacked any wall hangings or other artwork to relieve the gloom. There was no air conditioning, although fresh air was available via an ancient wire mesh grille that covered the diminutive window. There was neither in-room television nor telephone, although it did offer the luxury of a radio that supplied a menu of government-sanitised news and aged BBC programmes. There was no radio guide, and listening was extremely frustrating as all of the very few available channels switched from English to Afrikaans every couple of hours, and at different times each day, even in mid programme.

I cannot testify to the detail of other rooms in the hotel, as I was never offered the choice. Apparently, according to the bigoted and bloated housekeeper of the time, this was because 'Mr Key likes Room 2, which was certainly news to me.

Although I am critical of the place, I developed a sort of love-hate relationship with it, and it generated much humour. In those days, predating mobile phones and, before I discovered international phone cards, the only way to phone out was to use the payphone in the darkly lit corridor (several light bulbs had expired long before my initial visit and seemed destined to remain in situ forever). This only took five-cent coins (less than 1p, even then), and the only way to make it accept each of the multitude required was to pick up the whole instrument, insert a coin (in near darkness), and bang it down on the table sharply. Needless to say, I made few calls, especially as international calls between South Africa and the United Kingdom were then amongst the most expensive in the world.

A second ritual that I never managed to master was that of early morning tea. I much prefer to get up quietly and wait until breakfast time for my first refreshment of the day, but after several stays, I learned that I could have tea or coffee, but that nothing was certainly not an option. Morning tea was served always on the early side of the time requested by a bellboy resplendent in a dirty khaki boiler suit much as worn by a garage mechanic. Indeed, there was every possibility that it had already been used as such. He would bang loudly on the door to announce his arrival. To meet such room service was a considerable shock to the system in the early hours. The final part of the procedure was the recovery of the tea tray, which followed fairly swiftly upon its delivery, but irrespective of my early morning routine, always just as I stepped under the shower.

My last visit to the Meyerton was in winter. Arriving after dark, I was duly booked into Room 2. A colleague helped me with my luggage. In the dark corridor, I opened the door with relative ease, and then groped along the wall for several feet for a light switch. Having illuminated the room, my host enquired as to why I had totally shunned the entryway light. I replied that it did not work and nor had it done so for my past half dozen trips, confirming this with a demonstration. This resulted in a review of hotel accommodation in the surrounding area, and I moved from the sublime to the ridiculous in the form of a recently refurbished hotel offering superb accommodation, albeit at the cost of a longer journey to work each day. My only misgiving here was the security guard who greeted us warmly each evening—he knew my hosts well, they had dismissed him from their employment for theft. To this day, I find it curious that the white minority find it more acceptable to protect themselves and their possessions from the black majority by employing black security guards, who have every reason to dislike them, rather than demean themselves by engaging in such lowly work.

To enter the production facilities of the company with which I consulted, it was again necessary to shower several times. In the apartheid days, it was quite natural to have separate showers, not for male and female, but for black and white. As management became more enlightened, this was changed, such that the showers were reallocated to workers and management, respectively, with surprisingly little effect upon their use. It took the fast approaching end of apartheid to finally allocate the showers to male and female.

These distinctions were only a part of the problem of the showering process. Explanation of their purpose and use was hampered by a structure, where a Scotsman ran the company with a Dutch production manager, Afrikaans speaking managers, and a workforce that spoke a couple of native languages and understood little else. In addition, electrically controlled taps to prevent staff dodging the process were of little use in the face of a temperamental water supply, which, mercifully, usually protected one from a cold shower on those freezing winter mornings. The whole situation demanded huge expertise in the area of human relations, something that was at an almost primeval level of development in South Africa at that time. Apart from a considerable ability for dismissing black staff at whim, they confined their efforts to such vital activities as controlling the flow of executives through the corporate dining room of head office by insisting that those with even numbered telephones dined first, with odd numbers dining an hour later. As things progressed towards the end of apartheid, they found a need to learn about ethnic culture and integrate these revelations into management practice.

For some unknown reason, the ritual of showering is believed by many employed within the world's livestock industries to confer a complete inability of those so anointed to transfer disease to the animals under their protection. The more showers that one can cram into an employee's work schedule the better, and this is particularly important for the most menial of employees. Whilst showering may be a valuable asset to any bio-security programme, many of its advocates use it as the sole control and in tandem with other practices that are guaranteed to encourage spread of disease. Nowhere was this more true than South Africa, and when disease struck, it was always deemed to be the fault of the hapless workers who were often summarily dismissed, presumed guilty, without evidence, of avoiding the showers. Management, who were always patently guilty of lack of common sense and often also of gross negligence, routinely escaped censure. The usual remedy of management, after such a failure, was to add even more showers into the ritual. One enterprising organisation instigated a procedure where access to its facility was via a dip tank straddled by a wall, which extended down well below the surface of the water. To encourage compliance, a guard (again black) with a machine gun sat observing its use. All went swimmingly until it was discovered that someone had defecated in the tank, much to the horror of the white management who then hurriedly abandoned the whole idea.

Although still very much a junior member of my own company's management team, foreign travel introduced me to the ritual of corporate board meetings, again due to the ancient premise that anyone who has arrived on the big silver bird from the other side of the world must be important. Prior to ever attending such an event, I had high hopes as to the anticipated display of intellect and decisiveness to be witnessed, but these hopes were seldom fulfilled. South African board meetings were a case in point.

Preparation for these board meetings was impressive. Heaps of lengthy documents were photocopied and distributed in neat folders, keeping several secretaries in a spin for days. The most impressive thing of all was the care taken to get to the meeting on time, or so I thought. The general manager, Bill Wallace, uncharacteristically bedecked in suit and tie would insist on departing on the forty-five minute drive to head office an impressive three or four hours before the meeting was due to commence. As we approached our destination, all became clear, and we had to stop for lunch. This was not to be just a mere sandwich, but a major meal, prefaced by a couple of gin and tonics, and accompanied by a bottle of good wine. Bill knew that he was about to be ritually abused for several hours and that, as that outcome was certain, he preferred to be comfortably anaesthetised throughout the entire process.

In this fortified state, we were well prepared to enter the hallowed portals of the head office. Although outposts, like that occupied by Bill and his team, were relatively sparse, South African Corporate bunkers of the time vied with one another in their opulence and quota of original artwork, even in businesses on the verge of bankruptcy where they served to isolate their incumbents from the realities of life. When one is knee deep in pile carpet, staring at impressive works of art, it is hard to think that one's world is about to end. In this way, they served much the same purpose as Bill's excessive lunches. We would thus sink into the suffocating comfort of the anteroom and await our call to the presence.

The whole proceedings were conducted with gentlemanly courtesy, much like some religious ritual, officiated over, not by a high priest or bishop, but by an elderly and very senior executive, regaled in pinstripe suit and almost throttled by his tie, which was skewered in place, just below his Adam's apple, by a vicious tiepin. His role was to oversee the intonation of accounts and reports and then to observe the sport of his acolytes harassing poor Bill. This having been done to his complete satisfaction and safe in the knowledge that no significant decisions had been taken he would close the meeting and retreat to his sanctuary. The rest of the attendees would then repair to a good restaurant for drinks and dinner prior to Bill driving me back to my hotel. Happily, his performance at the wheel of a car was not seriously handicapped by this well-practiced ordeal.

Customer visits were an essential component of each visit, and Bill always put together a formidable itinerary of these for each of my visits. The customer base ran the full gamut of the white population from a large number of ageing British expats to Afrikaners, who were almost always excellently trained. This training was usually in veterinary medicine, which, in South Africa, conferred upon them the title of 'doctor', almost always along with an assumption of something approaching papal infallibility, which made it particularly pleasurable to engage them in technical argument. All these good people shared two common passions. The first of these, which was fairly manageable, was a love of rugby. This, on occasions, necessitated me watching a game. Given my school experience, this was just about tolerable. The second, much more enjoyable, but infinitely more dangerous passion, was an encyclopaedic knowledge of South Africa's excellent wines along with an unquenchable thirst for them at any time when two, or more, were gathered together. This was actively encouraged and shared in by Bill, which would have been fine, except for the fact that I was usually totally dependent upon him for transportation back to my hotel many miles away.

On occasions, I would be invited to spend weekends staying with customers, which was almost always pleasurable and provided a pleasant relief from the Meyerton's table d'hôte menu. Often, this was with one of the expat British community, which brought with it the hazard of being expected to consume vast quantities of alcohol. One such weekend commenced with addressing a customer seminar in Pietermaritzburg before lunch. I was relieved that lunch was only accompanied by a small beer. Unfortunately, I then discover that the afternoon was to be dedicated to sampling South Africa's impressive array of red wines. Some six or seven hours later, I was handed over to my host for the weekend. He had clearly partaken of the afternoon's activity rather more enthusiastically than I had. As he led me to his gleaming new SUV, he boasted of its many features, which included an anti-hijack device. This was designed to sense the driver being yanked out of his seat and responded by immobilising the vehicle and activating numerous alarms. This Roy explained was a vital accessory, especially in this particular area due to the current high number of hijackings. We set off on our thirty-mile journey to Roy's home at a rather faster speed than was comfortable to me, bearing in mind that, apart from Roy's condition, it was pitch black and foggy. Roy leant forward in his seat and, to my initial relief, the car came to a grinding halt with lights flashing and horns blaring. Roy's attempt at seeing where he was going had shifted most of his weight off the seat and triggered the anti-hijack device. After a few minutes of reflection, I realised that moving towards home, even with Roy in his befuddled state, was probably safer than being sitting ducks to any local terrorists. The only impediment to resuming our journey was that Roy had no idea where the reset button was hidden, and we thus spent the next half hour, groping around all the most unlikely areas of the vehicle's upholstery until we found the carefully hidden switch and resumed our journey. It has to be said that on arrival at Roy's home, we received an exceptionally frosty welcome from his normally charming wife and bedtime was declared immediately, with no offer of dinner or anything else. However, by breakfast time, all was forgiven, and we were each presented with a can of beer, which set the alcoholic tone for the day. It was only when back in the relative safety of Bill's hospitality that I was able to rehydrate.

The winds of change blowing through Africa certainly did not miss poor Bill. For many years, he had held his company together, with his amiability and the huge support and entertainment that he lavished upon his customers. As long as Bill had capable managers supporting him, all was well, but the pool of trained and talented middle managers became ever smaller as South Africa failed to continue to attract immigrants. In this situation, those changing companies either commanded huge salaries, were less than competent, or both. It was thus that Bill was let down by a considerable retinue of mediocre, but colourful, individuals. The worst of these rapidly gained the title of Captain Chaos with his customers. This was a richly deserved honour as this individual managed to wreak havoc wherever he chose to exercise his management skills. As economic conditions tightened and Bill's own low level of technical and managerial skills became increasingly apparent, the old formula failed to work and poor Bill was replaced, along with most of his management team.

The architect of Bill's demise was Rod Rockliffe, a man of great strategic vision who not only didn't take prisoners, but also could not conceive that there could be any possible reason forever doing so. Any manager who was not for his plan and demonstrably capable of executing it enthusiastically was dispensable. The corporate corridors frequently rang with his grim catch phrase 'we need a hanging', which inevitably prefaced the demise of yet another executive. It has to be said that Rod was the most effective change agent that I have ever met and left behind him a string of exceptionally well-run companies.

Rod's passion for excellence extended to his many hobbies, and it was pleasurable to be with him in the bush where he could demonstrate his extensive knowledge of African flora and fauna. This passion led to some tension, when travelling with him, as he kept the definitive tome on birds of southern Africa in his car. This book lists in excess of nine hundred birds and is complete with accompanying CD of their various calls. To educate me, and reinforce his own knowledge, he would play these on our various journeys, expecting me to follow the text and then prompting me to read out the description of each entry at the appropriate moment. Unfortunately, for me, especially when jet lagged, I rapidly fell asleep on long car journeys and demonstrated less than the required level of attention to this task. Nevertheless, I am grateful to him for the fact that I will never miss the call of the Ground Hornbill or mistake this unattractive looking bird for anything else.

For many years, I visited South Africa every six months or so, and it was fascinating to witness the social change that was going on, leading up to the inevitable end of apartheid and into the new South Africa led by the inspirational Nelson Mandela. At first, the white population generally did not dare contemplate what was happening, and over a period of fifteen or more years, they came to accept, reluctantly, that the good times were over and that they too could suffer the indignities of another race having the preferred rights to employment. Many seeing that their children face almost certain unemployment even when superbly qualified have dispatched them off to Europe for a few years. This has been to the considerable detriment of the British tourist industry where it is now common to be greeted by South African bartenders and waiters who combine their particular blend of forthrightness with a lack of practical skills and customer awareness bred of generations of being waited upon from the cradle. One can only hazard a guess at the internal trauma bottling itself up inside these poor unfortunates deprived of the wealth, comfort, and sunshine that was their birthright and forced into slavery in a foreign land. It is curious how time has a habit of balancing the wrongs of the past. Others are leaving their homeland forever and coming to terms with learning new skills such as ironing, cleaning, cooking, and human relations.

South Africa is a complex mixture of natural wealth, be it in the form of rare minerals or tourist potential, huge social problems, such as lack of education and the Aids epidemic, both brought about largely by its apartheid policies and huge opportunity. It is to be hoped that it can emerge from its current state of flux into a compassionate, democratic, and prospering nation.

CHAPTER 8

GOOD EVENING AMERICA

I was well prepared for my initial visit to America. Reared from an early age on a diet of weekly episodes of Perry Mason, many of the imperfections of Americans had been pointed out to me by my near relatives, especially my father. They had murdered the pronunciation of the English language and done even worse to its grammar and spelling. They were materialistic in the extreme and had ruined the tourist spots of Europe with their money, loudness, and general vulgarity. All this merely compounded their major crime of the century of coming into World War II at the last minute, and then claiming the victory for themselves and running off with our women. In many ways, they were infinitely worse than the Germans who, despite earlier misdemeanours, now restricted themselves to monopolising the deckchairs around the swimming pools of Europe.

My first serious encounter with American culture was provided by the ladies of Delta Airlines. In the mid-1980s, Delta's mentality was still very domestic in nature, and its cabin attendants, ageing first-generation stewardesses, mainly hailing from around its base city, Atlanta, of *Gone with the Wind* fame. Indeed, it could well have been that they had been in their prime in that era. I first realised that I was in America when challenged as to whether I would like coffee. The simple answer, 'Yes, white, please,' led to a blank stare, followed by the litany of questions, 'Regular or decaf?' 'With or without cream?' (to which the reply, 'No, I'd like milk, please,' merely caused confusion), 'Sugar or sweetener? (and, if so, which one?).' The clash of two cultures separated by a common language was then immediately obvious, as neither the age-weary cabin attendant nor I could see any humour in the situation. I have often considered drawing up a questionnaire in flow chart form which could be handed out with the immigration forms to alleviate much mental suffering to the likes of me when bombarded in such fashion when merely trying to obtain a simple cup of coffee, especially when half asleep. A further, yet to be encountered, challenge was to be the flavoured creamer, which can desecrate even the worst coffee. It is my view, and that of most of my fellow countrymen, that coffee should taste of coffee and not of plastic vanilla, or worst of all synthetic hazelnut.

If coffee presents its challenges, I was to learn that these are as nothing compared with those that I was to meet in the States, over the years, in my ongoing quest for a decent cup of tea. Common or garden tea has now been demoted to 'English Breakfast', or even 'Irish Breakfast', whatever that is and whatever differentiates it from the English variety. These take their place equally alongside camomile, peppermint, rose hip, and so forth, in terms of supermarket shelf space. I have long believed that in this arena there is a ready market for tea of any obscure-sounding origin, the more bizarre the better, and my personal suggestion of a winner would be 'skunk and bilberry.' As an aside, the failed flavours could find a ready market in the hair shampoo industry wherever more bizarre concoctions meet instant success. Why, having gone to much trouble to shower one's self, should the smearing one's hair and body with concoctions, extracted from fruit juices, improve the situation remains unclear to me. However, returning to the subject of tea, having chosen your variety of tea, one's problems are only just beginning, especially in the air, where it is normal to be presented with lukewarm water, heated and tainted in a well-used coffee jug, a tea bag, and artificial cream. The ensuing beverage represents an unpleasant combination of tastes and discarded packaging, only being eclipsed in its nastiness by the substitution of powdered creamer for the liquid variety.

On rare occasions, one is lulled into a false sense of security by the appearance of a teapot. This always heralds tepid water, the pristine teabag nestling by the side of the pot promising even greater disappointment. As an added bonus, it is a virtual certainty that the teapot will spew its contents all over the table from its various orifices when one attempts to pour its offending contents into a cup. Why those who supply the US catering industry haven't mastered the art of designing a teapot, or made an accurate copy of this everyday English item, is hard to understand. Needless to say, after about twenty years of fruitless search, I have given up and now only drink tea, brewed from personally imported teabags, within the safe confines of my own home.

At this early stage, however, most of this was to be experienced long into the future and, as we landed in Atlanta, I was about to experience the unimaginable; an airport that really worked. It must be abundantly clear to all, with the exception of British politicians and the executives of the British Airports Authority, that the best thing to do with Gatwick and Heathrow airports is to abandon them, borrow the blueprint for Atlanta, and start afresh in the Thames estuary, even if this does disturb a very few rare species of failed wildlife for a very short time. Perhaps it is impossible for one nation to master both the skills of tea making and airport designing.

Once again, the immigration clerks gave clues to the national character or at least, that of the Deep South. As long as one vigorously respected the yellow line in the immigration hall and had filled in the forms in a tidy fashion, they were, and still are, generally friendly and polite. Having negotiated immigration and customs and being reunited with my luggage in less than fifteen minutes (something that is probably against the law in Britain), I was free to enjoy the wonders of the airport, and especially the underground transit, which connected the various terminals with amazing speed. I came to welcome the disembodied voice, which told you where you were and the machine gun noise, which deterred those delaying the train's departure by standing in the doorways. Regrettably, both have now been replaced by more politically correct, but less effective, messages and sounds.

After a brief, but uncomfortable, commuter plane ride, I was at my destination, Huntsville, Alabama. Stepping from the plane, my first encounter with the American outdoors on that late June evening was a breath depriving, energy sapping, wall of humid heat, replaced moments later by the chilling balm of the arrival building's air conditioning. Although the airport was then small and unsophisticated, it became immediately apparent from the decor that we were ensconced in the space industry and that this was indeed a high-tech city. The bright lights of the myriad of fast food joints served only to emphasise this; after all Scotland, at that time only boasted one Dunkin Donuts and a couple of McDonald's, my then home town of Dunfermline finally getting its first store in January 1990, the same month as Moscow. Huntsville was not, however, my final destination, which turned out to be Athens, Alabama, located some twenty miles west and fifty years behind.

This journey was also my first encounter with the ubiquitous Ford Crown Victoria, a vehicle which combines a gargantuan external appearance with an interior of exceedingly modest proportions with all the sagging comfort of a small Victorian lounge. This vehicle is the exact opposite of *Doctor Who's Tardis*, where modest external dimensions give way to a vast interior. Nowhere is this more true than in the boot (or trunk), so designed as to only accept one normal-sized suitcase, and this only after a considerable struggle. The handling of the vehicle also harks back to Victorian times, but its indestructible nature led to the examples that I first met being the backbone of the taxi trade some twenty years later.

That evening I made my first acquaintance with my first American motel and marvelled at the size of the rooms and of the beds, a far cry from the cramped discomfort of most budget hotels in Britain. The most reassuring feature of this abode was that all rooms were identical, down to the picture on the wall of each room (depicting a cotton field in bloom), so one could never have any doubt as to where one was. Otherwise, the place had no redeeming features at all, unless one liked to swim in the pool, situated in the middle of the car park and surrounded by asphalt (or blacktop as the locals called it).

The motel was, somewhat inappropriately, named the 'Welcome Inn.' The motel's tradition was to formally welcome its most important guest of the day on its illuminated roadside sign. Despite many visits, I was destined never to be so honoured, always being outranked by others. There was a strong pecking order for this dubious honour, headed by visiting Southern Baptist ministers, followed by country and Western singers, with presidents of major client companies a very distant third. Apart from the sign, any welcome was cursory in nature and basically designed to elicit whether or not one was likely to be able to pay the bill.

The place at that time enjoyed a healthy monopoly in the locality, which circumvented any need to invest in even vestigial attempts at customer care. This was best illustrated by the mystery of the shrinking shirts. At breakfast, one morning, a colleague and fellow traveller confessed that he was putting on weight so drastically during his trip that he could no longer fasten the top button of his shirt without risk of strangulation. This seemed strange to me as I was experiencing similar discomfort myself. Being deeply analytical by nature, I was quickly able to ascertain to our joint and considerable relief that we had both subjected our shirts to the motel's laundry service. Thus, armed with the facts, which nobody would be able to dispute, we faced Bob, the motel owner who accepted our story without challenge, 'Funny thing, that! D' ya know, I had the same trouble, so I stopped using the service and now send my shirts to a little woman round the corner. She does a much better job, and I haven't had that problem since I started using her.' With that the conversation was abruptly terminated, and he turned his attention to another customer.

Athens at that time was, and still is more than twenty years later, a sleepy southern town. The main national stores had long ago forsaken their downtown sites in favour of grander stores along the main highways, leaving their previous sites as gloomy and faded monuments to their past retail glory.

The options for eating were largely confined to an impressive array of fast food outlets and a Chinese restaurant, which never appeared to open. The non-opening restaurant was an expanding trend; one local restaurant, having built a thriving lunchtime business, decided to limit its offering to evenings as it was far too much of an inconvenience for the owner to continue to open at lunchtime when its clientele really valued it. The main reason for the paucity of real restaurants was the fact that Athens was situated in a dry county and would continue thus as long as the ministers of the local churches continued to have their stranglehold over the local community. It is unfortunate that, however good the food, no proper restaurant had been able to survive, leaving the local population with the daunting choice of fast food or catfish. Most succumbed to the lure of good eating and drinking in Huntsville, twenty miles away, and ran the gauntlet of the drink-drive laws and possible humiliation in the local newspaper alongside the school lunch menu for the week. To an Englishman, like myself, the juxtaposition of apologies for drink-driving offences, invitations to partake of goat stew in the name of charity, and the school meals menu for the week was both novel and curious.

For the first few visits, deprived of transport, and a newcomer to fast food, I survived on a menu of burgers and soda, only breaking out every two or three days and having a meal on a real plate.

The 'eat as much as you like' buffets, however, rapidly lost their novelty, especially when one was expected to mix jello (jelly to an Englishman), fruit, and main course on the same plate and dine in the company of the regulars whose bulk attested to the ad-libitum possibilities of such establishments. Sometimes I would eat at the Welcome Inn, which has led to an aversion to the inevitable prime rib, served with its regulation slice of dyed apple (why should artificially coloured red apple flesh be thought to be more appetising than the natural state?).

As relative novices to international travel, and very aware of the delicate nature of our American subsidiary, we were probably not demanding enough of our American colleagues when it came to our living and transportation arrangements. In hindsight, it probably gave them some weird sense of security to know exactly where we were and to only let us out to their chosen restaurants when chaperoned by at least two of their number, but it certainly limited our appreciation of the area in those early days.

CHAPTER 9

GOOD MORNING AMERICA

And so to work, American style! It came as something as a shock to find that normal starting time was 8.00 a.m. and that, in the blazing heat of summer, anything requiring out of the ordinary exertion might even start at 4.00 a.m. to avoid the heat of the midday sun, something seldom, if ever, experienced back home. Even more surprising was the fact that, on the way to work at such a start time, one might find little old ladies enjoying the over easy and bacon (not to mention the grits) at a local roadhouse. The very mention of grits strikes horror into my soul; every maize-growing nation has its own form of culinary hell from the African 'mealie pap' to the American grits; all a weak imitation of Scottish oats-based porridge. In addition, America manages to add gravy to the list of breakfast options. This glutinous grey sludge fails to improve flavour, nutritional excellence, or eye appeal of the breakfast plate, but is successful in helping to condemn many to the tender care of the cardiologist at an early age.

An early impression of the rural workplace was that most of the men wore baseball caps, both indoors and out. Was this some strange religious cult or even something more sinister? As the years progressed, the answer became blindingly obvious; to venture outside into the Alabama sun when follicularly challenged was a sure way to instant sunburn, or worse. The only time when heads were bare was when their owners were dressed for formal occasion (usually church). To meet a colleague thus attired and capless for the first time was something of a shock. Who was this balding person advancing towards one with such familiarity?

On arrival at work, I was amazed to find how positive and respectful everyone was. On enquiring as to someone's health, the very worst condition they would admit to was, 'Good, thank you,' and that represented a near terminal state of health. One could relax at 'marvellous' or 'fabulous', but the British norm of a noncommittal 'OK' would have been grounds for calling in the emergency services. Regrettably, this same enthusiasm could be used to lull one into a sense of wellbeing when disaster was actually about to strike, as it was all too often.

The company, as I walked into it on the first day, was in a sorry state having just lost its president, a big talking American from the Deep South, who had ruled this offshoot of a British company in the manner of a sometimes-benevolent dictator of some minor South American state, enthusiastically supported by his wife and personal assistant. This was the reason for the sudden visit of myself and several colleagues from head office. Most able individuals fed up of being told their opinions and refusing to honour their president, had either sought alternative employment or been fired. Those that remained were well used to maintaining a low profile and either painstakingly avoiding their president, or attending to his every whim. A key part of their survival strategy had been to provide their British parent company with as little information as possible in the hope that they would be left alone. It was therefore not surprising that the only information readily to hand was the manual of instruction for the cleaning of the offices, and this only if one had access to the dark recesses of the ladies' restroom. The president's office merited four pages of detail concerning daily, weekly, and monthly protocols, the rest of the building merited one solitary paragraph. Needless to say, this had all been drawn up by the president's wife.

The immediate task at hand was to keep things running and, after a week of apparently gaining enthusiastic agreement to various action plans, our team departed for home in a state of euphoria, returning some weeks later to find that absolutely nothing had happened in the intervening period. It was clear that this team needed more leadership than we could provide by our intermittent visits and our urgent focus then became the search for a new president. This obviously meant hiring a dependable

Brit who could be relied upon to understand the eminently sensible and unchallengeable requests of the owners and have them implemented in Alabama. This was, somewhat surprisingly, achieved almost immediately with a minimum of effort. At about this time, and having spoken to many British businessmen involved in similar ventures, I began to wonder how on earth the British Empire ever got off the ground, its demise was certainly no chance occurrence.

The new company president, Edward Whinning, took up the challenge with gusto. Within days, he was blinding his British masters with a profound knowledge of the local language, referring to the acquisition of trucks and farm equipment in obscure terms that nobody in Scotland had ever heard of, and had repainted all the trucks, irrespective of age or condition, in a new corporate livery of his own creation. These clever actions, eagerly reported to head office, suggested intense action whilst masking the fact that the same non-existent level of communication was taking place on all matters of significance, as had been the hallmark of the previous regime. This was successful in keeping the owners at bay, at least for a while. Other signs of 'going native' should have been worryingly evident: the acquisition of a large purple gas guzzling monster of a company car, clad in velour, rather in the style of a cheap Victorian lounge suite, and the purchase of not only one, but also several mini tractors for personal use.

Urged to strengthen the management team, he offered up one candidate, Wayne Dinkum for approval by head office. Wayne's trip to the United Kingdom did not start well. Armed with his new passport, and never before having left the United States of America, he was, not surprisingly, overwhelmed by Gatwick Airport. One could understand any difficulty he may have had with the interminable and hostile immigration process, but why he could not differentiate between the male and female toilets is still unclear to this day. Having accidentally entered the ladies' toilets, and hearing female steps behind him, he bolted into a cubicle and then, with great presence of mind, raised his feet high off the floor every time he imagined approaching footsteps. In fear of being thrown in jail, or more likely deported on the next plane home as a potential sex offender, he remained in his self-inflicted incarceration long enough to miss his connecting flight to Edinburgh. This set the backdrop to his interview, which was not a success. Given the thumbs down by the whole United Kingdom team, his appointment was, somewhat predictably, confirmed by the president upon Wayne's return to Alabama.

It was then, and is, even now, a considerable surprise to meet the wives of men like Wayne. Where Wayne suffered from the 'short man' syndrome, making up for his lack of height and looks with an aggressive nature, his wife was attractive, charming, and intelligent; not that anyone would dare to take advantage of her, given Wayne's continual mention of his weight training and of the extensive gun collection that he displayed prominently in their home. Wayne's wife was named Harmony, one of the few occasions where parents had successfully anticipated the character that their new charge would ultimately develop. It seems, to me, provocative, and tempting fate in the extreme, to give one's child a name such as Joy, Precious, Harmony or Constance, let alone Chastity.

Poor Wayne didn't last long; his considerable ego could not survive against that of Edward Whinning, and he was very soon being mentioned adversely in dispatches to head office and was, in similar manner to his hiring, summarily dismissed by the local management, again contrary to the advice of head office who urged caution in this process.

This time, determined to get it right, the head office team decided to involve itself in the recruitment process from the start, hiring not one, but four vice presidents—for production, finance, sales, and quality, respectively. The process started with the development of interminable lists of potential questions to pose to the lucky applicants, a local Alabama headhunter was briefed, and we awaited the response—which came in the form of hundreds of perfect curriculum vitas.

This was an early learning point—even in those early days of the personal computer, every American could generate a grammatically correct and perfectly spelt application and was well capable of making the most of their virtues, however, few these may be. Four thousand miles away in Scotland, few of their transatlantic cousins were this capable (which at least had the advantage of making the process of identifying candidates for interview there much easier). Eventually, the shortlists were made, with the help of the headhunter, who was surprisingly adept at agreeing with our inspired selection of candidates for interview.

The interviews were then carried out, and we complimented ourselves on the wonderful talent we had amassed. Even those candidates who were currently out of work had excellent reasons for this unhappy state, which usually centred on them having identified amazing opportunities for improving labour efficiency and then, after implementing the necessary staffing cuts, having selflessly fallen on their swords and added themselves to the list of casualties. When asked to outline their strengths, most candidates could go on for hours. Fortunately, their weaknesses were few, usually restricted to confessions of a tendency to work too many hours or to fail to make full use of their meagre vacation allocation. Some questions were answered with remarkable frankness. One production candidate when asked what he believed the role of quality controllers to be replied that they were 'like the teats on a boar, present, but with absolutely no function'.

Eventually, we identified the best candidates and made job offers, which were wisely refused by the really intelligent ones, who could not face living in such a location, and for a company, which at that time had little to commend it in terms of facilities, investment plans, or track record. Finally, we achieved our team of four and put them to the work of running the company, headed up by Edward Whinning, which would have been fine, except they hated one another and him, with a passion.

The new team comprised of: VP of finance, Doug Dollar; VP of sales, Patrick D. Flaherty; VP of production, Angus Mac Phee; and VP of quality, Ben Hectare. Of these, all were American, and unknown, with the exception of Angus Mac Phee who, not surprisingly, hailed from Scotland and with whom I had worked in Wiltshire at the very start of my career.

Angus Mac Phee's main characteristic was that he was, as the Scots say, 'careful' with his money—and, for that matter, also with that belonging to anyone else. This was the major reason for the success of his career, which had started with a lengthy spell with a company where bankruptcy was never far away from knocking on the door, but which he successfully kept at arm's length by his economy with his employers' very limited resources. Not for him the luxuries of an expense account—a sandwich in a pub car park, or in the United States, the bounty of a drive through window, was more than adequate for him and any poor unfortunates who happened to be with him. He was proud that all his projects came in below budget, but he was amazingly adept at creating those very budgets and generous in surreptitiously bequeathing chunks of cost to others, often to their considerable surprise many months later when they discovered his benevolence.

Even Angus was not immune from the vagaries and imprecision of construction estimates, which sometimes would not even be contained within his substantial padding. It was not uncommon for the hapless manager of one of Angus' new units to find that his office was bereft of even the barest essentials of furniture, such as a desk and a chair, in order that Angus could maintain his proud boast of always being on budget. His pièce de résistance, however, was a toilet cum showering facility that threatened his reputation severely. The divisions between stalls were to be constructed out of eight-foot by four-foot sheets of material, and he stretched ingenuity beyond the limit by making two divisions out of each sheet. This was barely satisfactory in the showers where, installed at a suitable height, a four-foot division could protect the modesty of a standing incumbent—although it offered a tempting challenge to limbo dancers. Four-foot high toilet stall divisions, however, could in no way offer privacy, especially so when combined with doors created out of translucent shower curtains.

Happily, for him, but to the chagrin of others, Angus enjoyed a phenomenal memory. It was like an instant-recall-dictating machine that could relate any conversation in the last ten years verbatim, neatly date stamped for additional convenience. This was merely annoying when he expected one to be able to recite anecdotes in similar manner. However, it was deadly when he was explaining one of his mystery bequests as he could muster all his facts and conveniently invent others to suit his case whilst one was desperately searching one's brain cells to recall an incident which may, or may not, have happened in the dim and distant past. Further, he believed that information was power, and treated it in exactly the same manner as his money, keeping it close to his chest and avoiding sharing it with another soul if at all possible.

Being an advocate of the simple life, Angus had little time for 'ethnic' foods (which included all American food in his personal definition.). All his regular meals had to be denuded of dressings, pickles, etc, something that caused instant confusion in the average fast food outlets, and he always politely declined the opportunity to eat Chinese, having 'done it once.'

Doug Dollar was entirely different; tall, suave, and well dressed, whereas, Angus was introspective and shabbily conservative in his appearance and persuasive even in the total absence of facts. Where Angus had to rely on his formidable left-brain to support him, Doug assumed the role of the company authority on American business practices, particularly concerning employment conditions, where he went to great lengths to attempt to educate his ignorant British superiors. Apparently, most Americans in enlightened companies not only enjoyed better salaries, but also more generous pensions and vacations than their transatlantic British counterparts. Doug always wore impeccably laundered shirts, had two perfect children, a perfect wife, and, unfortunately, an unhealthy interest in the sex lives of female members of staff. This would ultimately lead to his downfall, but for now, he merely got under the skin of his colleagues by virtue of his superior attitude and well-developed capacity for stabbing people in the back.

Patrick D. Flaherty, of distant Irish descent, can best be summed up in the phrase Leonard Hughes, the Irish dramatist, used to describe Ireland itself, 'full of genius, but with absolutely no talent'. He was likeable, intelligent, and talked a good fight, but was outsmarted and intimidated by his colleagues and achieved little.

The brilliant Ben Hectare likewise achieved very little, but contributed considerable guile and deceit to the team. He was also adept at blackmailing the company into allocating him ever more resources and staff, with the threat that, unless his requests were met, he could not meet the legal minimum of standards and all of us would end up in jail. All this was, however, driven by an overzealous, almost manic, personal ambition and a belief that he could walk on water. When he, and others, discovered that he couldn't even float, he rapidly crumbled, but this eventuality was still some time away.

It is not surprising that all of this presented their leader, Edward Whinning with a considerable challenge. To integrate new blood into a well-established team is always tough, but attempting to coordinate this bunch into the dream team was more like a nightmare, especially as the pressure from the marketplace, and the owners, to get the company to perform were intense and increasing. He, therefore, decided that he had to take the initiative and take his team away for a blue sky meeting.

Whilst Edward was preparing for this momentous event, a preparation that mainly centred upon the catering arrangements, he declined to attend a corporate blue sky meeting in Scotland, pleading the need to be with his subordinates. He had been in business long enough that he should have known that the ready acceptance of this submission signalled imminent personal danger, and, sure enough, the overwhelming conclusion of the corporate meeting was that Edward must be replaced without delay.

Very soon after this, the team from head office descended on Alabama to implement this decision. The task was made all the more difficult as Edward was, as they arrived, at the wheel of his huge camper van with his team on board, departing for one of the first and only phoneless and peripatetic blue sky meetings ever to be conducted. As they had enough food on board to feed an army, and as their destination was not known to anyone, all the contingent from head office could do was to wait for the camper van to return from the backwoods of Alabama. It began to look as if it had become the automobile equivalent of the Marie Celeste, doomed to roam the roads of Alabama for eternity with Edward and his crew on board, avoiding their ultimate fate. However, many hours later, Edward and his team returned to base, pleased with their day of bonding, planning, and eating. They expressed pleasure at unexpectedly bumping into their colleagues from Scotland. Regrettably, this pleasure was short lived, and Edward left his office for the last time.

It was early December, the weather was uncharacteristically warm, even for Alabama and for some unknown reason I felt it necessary, a couple of hours later, to visit Edward at home to empathise with him. As I rang his doorbell and heard the steady advance of his footsteps, I was aware of the warmth of the sun and the clear blue sky, so different to the dreary Scottish winter. As Edward opened the door, conversation was decidedly lacking, the deafening silence apparently stretching into eternity. I had to break it somehow 'hasn't it been a wonderful day?' I ventured, adding 'the weather, I mean', and hoped, in vain, that my insensitive gaffe had gone unnoticed. Thus compromised, I was hardly in any position to block his next request, which was that the management's

Christmas party should go ahead as a chance for him to say goodbye to his friends and colleagues.

The venue for this elite gathering was a local, grandly named, 'country club', which fell below expectation from first glimpse. Inside was a white grand piano attempting to bask in its former glory. Seated at it was a well known and capable singer/pianist who entertained us as best as she could, hampered by the fact that a fair proportion of the piano's notes didn't work. Whether the budget could not stretch beyond the first hour, or whether she, wisely, decided to give up the impossible I do not know, but the only musical instrument remaining after that time was a weary jukebox. As the glutinous meal thankfully came to its end, Edward's moment came. He stood up in the centre of the dance floor and gushingly thanked everyone for making his time with the company so enjoyable. At this, Doug Dollar, who had done nothing but undermine him from the start, rushed up to him and threw his arms around him. At the same moment, one of the secretaries hurriedly fed quarters into the juke box and it burst forth with Lara's theme tune from *Dr Zhivago's*, 'Somewhere my Love . . .' This was the perfect conclusion to the hypocrisy.

Now the Famous Four, Doug Dollar, Patrick Flaherty, Angus Mac Phee, and Ben Hectare were on their own with every opportunity to show their mettle. Innate capability plus their intense hatred of one another was all that could hold them back. To spur them on, their chairman, safely, as they thought, located in the United Kingdom and famous for his hatred of travel, airports, and airlines announced that he would take personal day-to-day responsibility for the American company.

CHAPTER 10

WHILST THE CAT'S AWAY

Jonathan Rampsbeck was not the typical British captain of industry. He was a staunch Yorkshireman and proud of it. Through his enviable scientific skills and intense fear of failure, he had transformed the company and its product range and thus set it on the road to outstanding success. His reward for this was to lead the company to ever-greater heights of success for the best part of twenty years during which time, especially latterly, he found himself working further and further away from the issues, which really motivated and inspired him. Apart from his gritty Yorkshire determination, he had those other hallmarks of his native county; blunt insensitivity, the ability to call a spade a spade, and contempt for anything or anyone that he considered to be even slightly phoney. He was far more at home having a quiet (or not so quiet) drink with his mates than fine dining with his peers from the corporate world. Added to this an enthusiasm for innovations, some brilliant and some positively barking mad plus the lowest boredom threshold imaginable and one might glean an inkling of the challenge facing most of us in our day-to-day interactions with him.

Although in no way racist, he had an enormous array of jokes in his universally dreaded 'joke book,' most of which amply demonstrated his forthright lack of sensitivity. As an example, he relished in repeatedly telling his favourite 'Hitler' joke to Gerhard, the German head of one of our European subsidiaries. This related to the Fuhrer's alleged attempts to get his scientists to convert excrement into butter, and their final admission that they could only improve the spreading ability, and do nothing concerning taste or smell. Jonathan was repeatedly perturbed by Gerhard's look of puzzlement and his failure to find any humour in any of Jonathan's many repetitions of this awful joke.

Jonathan had travelled widely throughout his business career, yet had never conquered the practicalities of international travel. Not for him any of the tricks, such as changing one's watch to local time, going to bed at 'local' bedtime, or possibly, eating and drinking very lightly for the first day or so to minimise the effects of jet lag. The outcome of this was usually a formidable agenda for the trip, exhaustion after the first day, acute gastrointestinal failure by the second, and then hasty review and an early flight home. Those of us who had worked with him for years could manage around this as a team and ensure that his desired outcome was achieved. Others, not so familiar with this routine were left in a state of total bewilderment.

Jonathan believed in keeping fit mainly by running. His running shoes were a constant source of complaint from those travelling with him, but they did allow for easy location of his motel room, both visually (as he placed them outside, underneath his window), and more potently, by their appalling smell which pervaded the not so immediate vicinity of his room. In addition, as with so many things, he tended to take his running to excess, which often left him semi-crippled and bereft of any form of benign composure.

In common with many travellers, he always suffered indigestion kept at bay by an impressive daily quota of antacid tablets. In addition, severe stomach upsets were a common occurrence. To go seeking one's chairman in the early morning when he failed to put in his usual over prompt attendance at breakfast, and for the knock on his door to be answered by six and a half feet of ashen white abject misery, dressed only in y-fronts is one thing. For the same vision (happily fully clad) to inform one in an aside whilst entering the hallowed portals of a South African boardroom, that his constitution was so desperately fragile that he was wearing a nappy, hand crafted out of toilet tissue, was guaranteed to detract one's attention from the agenda.

Gastrointestinal failure features highly in the experience of most international travellers and brings about much camaraderie. One unfortunate colleague joined us in Texas immediately after a foray into rural Mexico. On the five-hour road trip across Texas, we had to stop urgently, every half hour, at a gas station for him to relieve his desperate condition. Aspiring to the manner of an English gentleman, he refused to use the facilities until he had made some purchase, however slight. It was thus that he arrived at our destination a shadow of his former self, with much emptier bowels and a more than adequate supply of chewing gum. Despite our concern for him, at the time, his fellow travellers have enjoyed recounting this story, at his expense, for many years.

Faced with Jonathan's personality, and his usual jet-lagged condition, the Famous Four didn't stand a chance. Even at his lowest, he could easily outwit them, but they never saw, let alone appreciated his true brilliance and merely became more confused. Added to this, Jonathan's visits were merely a necessary nuisance to them, interfering as they did with their major priority of fighting one another. As they became less and less effective, other aspects of their characters also emerged.

Doug Dollar was the first to give cause for concern. He was able to get through the routine grind of finance very quickly. In common with the others, he ignored all issues involving leadership and cooperation with other departments completely. This left him bored and with a dangerous amount of time on his hands. His chosen distraction was a morbid curiosity concerning the personal lives of the female members of staff. Although, as with so much of what he did, it was probably all talk and no action, he succeeded in intimidating several of the female staff and alienating the rest.

Ben Hectare found ever more reasons to demand more resources to enhance product quality and increase his empire, surprisingly and unwittingly aided by Angus Mac Phee whose ever-more money pinching antics led to a spectacular and much denied decline in product quality. The essence of quality control is cooperation across departmental boundaries and focus on business processes. Such thinking was totally abhorrent to poor Angus who merely raised his defences and demanded blind loyalty from his subordinates. This was so successful that one of his lieutenants was able to boast in gushing tones to the head office team that quality was superb and had never been better, this at a time when the sales team was pleading to the most senior management of the company for something to be done. This individual was lucky to escape the interview without suffering grievous injury. Patrick Flaherty, who should have been leading the campaign to demand improve quality, had been successfully neutered by Angus and reduced to a whimpering wreck who could not even resolve such strategic issues as which secretaries should man the phone system at break times and where to go for lunch.

Faced with these shambles, Jonathan decided that it was time for some team building and, as usual, confident that he could work things out with little difficulty, set about arranging his own team-building course.

The chosen venue for this was a run-down vacation resort catering to the elderly, but situated in a spectacular rural location in Tennessee. Like so many of these places, the rooms were shabby, the service poor, and the menu predictably boring. Elderly Americans apparently don't like to stray far beyond poor quality, overcooked, meat chaperoned by watery green beans, broccoli, and instant mashed potato, washed down by iced tea, and finished off with industrial grade key lime pie. Things were so bad that the wife of one of the attendees was commissioned to smuggle in real food each evening.

The team-building sessions were loosely formatted to encourage the Famous Four to give written and verbal feedback on one another and the head office team. These sessions were interspersed with outdoor activities such as golf, horse riding, and even a visit to the local laser quest outlet to facilitate bonding.

The outdoor events went largely without incident. Doug looked imperial on his horse, whilst Angus looked totally miserable when engaged in any activity that he could not categorise as work to his full personal satisfaction. In this instance, this discredited most of the course content. Ben turned each activity into an Olympic competition (and probably practised each in advance for hours). Only laser quest generated true injuries, this when Jonathan, presumably not satisfied with harmlessly 'killing' Patrick with laser fire, propelled him into a brick wall with his not inconsiderable bulk. At the time, this was construed as an unfortunate accident, but only Jonathan really knows whether this was the case or whether sheer frustration finally got the better of him. Certainly, by all previous standards, Jonathan's patience had exceeded all bounds, up to this point, and the outcome provided the rest of us with a modicum of smug satisfaction.

The formal sessions were not a success. Whilst Jonathan could cope well with most competitive sports, gentle psychology was certainly not one of his core skills. In the first session, he asked the team to list their business frustrations, in an attempt to get into the problems inherent in their relationships. Angus filled not one, but five sheets with a mind-numbing list of all the capital items he required in order to be successful and ignored all reference to any other issues. Ben did likewise, in his case, demanding a huge list of laboratory gadgetry and the staff to run it all. Doug declared that he had no frustrations (or at least none that he would declare), and Patrick hadn't written a word by the end of the exercise. Frustration was definitely beginning to show in Jonathan, who decided to use the head-on approach (his usual and preferred course of action) for the next session. He thus introduced the session by telling them that they were the most dysfunctional apology for a management team that he had ever come across and that they would remain in the room until they had raised the true issues that were at the bottom of their failure to work as an effective team. There then followed one of the longest silences in the history of the company, only punctuated every quarter of an hour by the carillon outside chiming 'raindrops keep falling on my head,' which lent a quaintly surreal atmosphere to the whole grisly experience.

Eventually Jonathan, by now having shed all vestiges of patience and white with anger, gave up and headed for the airport with a face like thunder, leaving his colleagues to salvage the mess. His anger could hardly fail to be noticed, even by the Famous Four. Finally, after a few more work-related sessions, hastily patched together by the rest of us to fill in time, the course was declared over and they returned home, even more confused, hoping that it would be a long time before Jonathan braved their presence again.

Little did they know that Jonathan never gave up. Unable ever to sleep on a plane, he had first stocked up on antacids and in-flight alcohol and then written a lengthy brief for his favourite training consultant, a fellow Yorkshireman, Monty Steen. Monty had first come to his attention, some years previously, due to his reputation for reforming work teams that could best be described as basket cases. Jonathan, believing that this accurately described his then board of directors, had hired him instantly.

Jonathan's use of consultants within the parent company over the years had, much like his passion for innovation, introduced us to a range of talent ranging from the inspired to the barking mad. He always saw the prevailing need and attempted to fill the void with the best talent available.

Regrettably, the marketing efforts of consultants usually exceed their capabilities by a magnitude only rivalled by their fees. In the early years, priority was given to much needed time management, and once the evangelical zeal of some of the graduates of the course had subsided great progress was made. Even after accounting for the cost of personal investment in large enough briefcases to carry the voluminous and expensive planners that were the cornerstone of the system and which ensured ongoing revenue for their providers, most would admit to real improvements in their personal efficiency. The pocket diary of this system was of minimal appeal to me as it offered tiny spaces for each hour of the working day, which given the exceedingly limited legibility of my script, even when full sized, rendered it useless. It was impossible to criticise this volume, however, as Jonathan was its greatest proponent and extolled its virtues to all and sundry for at least ten years. This was unfortunate as the one certainty about him was that his diary bore no relation to reality, leading one of his colleagues to pick it up and introduce it as the greatest work of fiction in the English language. This was by no means solely the fault of the diary as it was entirely likely that Jonathan would go for days without reference to it, meanwhile making all manner of commitments that he would be unable to keep, even if his enthusiasm for them continued beyond this initial stage.

Jonathan's next target was business efficiency. Here, unusually, he had the full support of his fellow directors, all of whom could see the need to cut out waste. The chosen consultants had a formidably left-brained approach to life. This particularly appealed to the finance staff. It also appealed to the disaffected as, at its centre was the procedure of issuing caveats on other departments. The system demanded that these had to be responded to in writing, however stupid they may be. Although the bulk was sound and led to a much better organisation, a good ten per cent were such that common sense, so often, sadly, one of the scarcest resources in evidence in business, should have led to their rejection at an early stage. This would have saved much time and anger.

After this, it was time to pay attention to the more long-term issues, and here was where the choice of consultants became less successful. This was probably a direct consequence of the principle expounded by George Bernard Shaw that 'He who can, does. He who cannot, teaches,' but to which should be added, 'He who discovers, he can charge for it, consults.' The chosen candidate, Bill Watkins, was charismatic, had a huge list of prestigious companies on his client list and had published many books on just the topics that concerned us. In addition, he used buzz phrases like 'neurolinguistic programming', labels for techniques with which he promised to transform us. The clever thing about his approach, at least as far as he was concerned, was that, to gain the advantage promised by one course, he insisted that one had to follow it with another. In some ways, his offerings were like Chinese meals, where one is often hungry for more very soon after one has eaten enough to fear that one is in imminent danger of succumbing to acute indigestion, but in this case, the desire came from the cook rather than the diner. This was despite the fact that there was never a point at which one could identify a tangible benefit from any of his prior contribution.

Eventually, he was dropped, but even ten years on, he still phones and e-mails senior management, touting for business, blissfully unaware of his previous failure.

The absolute nadir was reached when a consultant masquerading under the role of 'industrial psychologist' was hired to give the board a three-day course on strategic thinking. It was clear from the beautifully crafted notes that he gave every participant that he actually only had one product, an extremely basic team-building course, and that he changed the front cover to meet the request of each client. He was also desperate to demonstrate his psychological skills, but far too dim to see that the hostility between a couple of participants in a role-playing exercise was entirely contrived. All that was gained from this ordeal was a couple of extremely nice lunches, considerable humour, and a grim determination never to use the man again.

Monty Steen had been employed extensively by the parent company. His team-building courses, although unconventional, had been life changing for some. The view of his work was varied. For those who wanted to change and gave their all to his programme, the results were remarkable and, as time wore on, it was those individuals, including Jonathan, who tended to be in the senior positions within the company. Regrettably, there were several, probably those who most needed to change, that only paid lip service to Monty's methods and were not influenced at all by the experience.

Jonathan judged that the American team wanted to change, but needed to be shown the way. This was his first mistake. The second was to inflict a British trainer, who had little experience of American culture, on three Americans and a Scotsman working in Alabama. Many excellent jokes are blessed with a less promising backdrop than this.

CHAPTER 11

A TIME FOR WORK

With his plans in place, but with the Famous Four only briefed to the extent of being instructed to keep certain dates free, Jonathan returned to America rather earlier than he had planned, and certainly much, much earlier than the Famous Four desired. All pleas, especially those emanating almost hourly from Angus, that pressure of work would prevent them from attending, as Jonathan mandated, were robustly rejected by him.

In a rare, and apparently conciliatory, move Jonathan did agree to arrive a couple of days early to inspect potential sites for Angus's newest project. It was thus that he travelled direct from the United Kingdom to deepest Arkansas in order to meet Angus and the site owners, first thing the next morning, at the remote field that was being proposed as the favourite site for the development. As is typical in small-town America, the possibility of attracting a foreign investment, promising dozens of jobs, caused considerable excitement and, much to Jonathan's consternation, a small crowd of local dignitaries, including the mayor and a sizeable delegation from the chamber of commerce were gradually assembling as the appointed hour approached. Overriding this consternation, Jonathan feared impending physical disaster. He had not travelled well and airline food was wreaking its well-practiced revenge upon his intestines. He needed a toilet urgently, and desperately whispered such to one of his aides. The result of this was that, after only having been introduced to a few of the dignitaries who had happened to arrive early, and before even these introductions were completed, the chairman was whisked away, by car, without word of explanation. He had gone in search of a restaurant, or any other facility possessing a 'restroom', as the Americans quaintly term it, although Jonathan's visit was to be anything but restful.

Immediately, and with surprised looks upon their faces, the assembled throng started enquiring, 'Where is he going?' This was, of course, a perfectly reasonable, but difficult, question to answer factually; one could hardly reply that the chairman was suffering acute diarrhoea and that we had no idea when, or whether, he would return. Happily after some minutes, which seemed to us like an eternity, spent stalling and giving vague answers like, 'I don't know, maybe he needs to make a phone call,' Jonathan returned and joined in the conversation as if he had been there all the time, probably leaving the locals muttering about differences in culture between the British and Americans.

Even when feeling well, Jonathan didn't excel in such situations. On several occasions, faced with the local elite, or with the senior partners of local businesses, he failed to meet up to their expectations. On one celebrated occasion, during Edward Whinning's presidency, a presentation of Edward's plans for a new corporate office was prepared, specifically for him, by the developer's senior architect. The brief had not been discussed in advance with Jonathan, but judging by his very visible enthusiasm for them, it was likely that the plans followed Edward's personal instruction to the architect in every detail. It may have been the provision of a personal restroom and a private exit for the president, direct from his lavish office suite to his adjacent personal parking spot that provoked Jonathan. I myself had only occasioned upon the concept of the private restroom for the chief executive once before, this in my youth when I was an altar boy in a cathedral. I never plucked up the courage to see what lay behind the oaken door resplendent with the word 'Bishop' gilded upon it in Gothic script.

If it was not the private restroom, it may have been the proposals for a vast and expensive plant atrium that annoyed Jonathan, but when the presentation concluded, Jonathan gave the bemused architect a withering look and left the room, again leaving the rest of the group to redeem the situation as best they could.

Having done his best to appease Angus, despite the difficult circumstances, and to encourage him onwards in his search for the perfect site, Jonathan and Angus set off together on the long journey to the location of the team-building course. It did little for their relationship that Angus received a speeding ticket en route. This was, according to Angus, who considered himself a consummate driver, totally due to a faulty cruise control mechanism which 'got stuck in the groove', whatever that meant. Jonathan didn't let up in his teasing for the whole journey, making them both desperately in need of some emergency team building by the end of the trip.

They arrived just in time for Monty Steen's introductory session. Despite having been recommended to dress casually, Angus, Patrick, and Ben all wore ties and sports jackets, and Doug was immaculate in his charcoal grey suit, white shirt, and matching red tie and braces. Jonathan was comfortably dressed in golf shirt and slacks. Much to the surprise of the Famous Four, their mentor, Monty Steen was dressed in a very casual shirt and jeans, his ensemble being completed by a pair of red loafers. In his hand, he held a pint of beer, and his casual conversation was punctuated with occasional well-chosen profanities. None of this sat well with Doug's Southern Baptist sensitivities nor with Angus's personal and somewhat straight-laced convictions. Patrick was undecided, and, as usual, Ben went along with things, hoping that he could gain personal advantage.

Doug immediately decided that he had to gain the upper hand and so began an interrogation of Monty to ascertain his academic credentials. To Doug's delight, and of absolutely no significance to Monty, he confirmed these to be few. Doug thus absolved himself of the need to take the course seriously and, foolishly, switched off.

Once the introductions were over, Monty suggested that, before dinner, they should relax, have a drink and, to break the ice, each draw a picture, depicting their individual perceptions of the team, and how it functioned. This immediately upset Angus, as he could not conceive that the drawing of any picture could possibly be categorised as work.

It was instantly clear from the resultant efforts that none of the team had a potential alternative career as an artist, but once each had explained his efforts, these revealed a lot about each member's thinking, and why the team was so dysfunctional.

Doug volunteered to go first. His picture portrayed a large bag with three individuals pouring money into it, and one, namely, Doug, preventing any of it from leaving the bag. It became crystal clear that it was Doug's belief that the others were to ensure all monies were passed up to the him and that he alone would dispense occasional crumbs of cash back to his colleagues as he thought fit to sustain the business. There was no indication that anyone outside the Famous Four was involved with the team nor that they had any form of accountability to their staff, superiors, or to the company.

Patrick's picture portrayed himself being held aloft by his peers, apparently indicating the need for all to support his sales efforts. This was similar in vein to Angus's portrayal of a complicated piece of machinery, surrounded by arrows pointing inwards towards it, indicating the need for all to blindly support this complex entity, which they could not possibly be expected to understand. Ben's very detailed drawing was of a water closet and, above it a large plunger, wielded by Ben, whilst others watched from the edge of the drawing. This, Ben explained, represented him being given free reign to purge the company's processes of all blockages without hindrance from anyone, in other words, he was the corporate plunger.

It was clear to Monty from this that the four of them, not only found it difficult to listen to a brief, but also that they had no concept as to how a team should operate. Each of them had focussed on their own function, and their own need for support, with no recognition that they might possibly need to support the others. With such introspection, it was hard to see how they could possibly be moulded into a winning team, even in embryo, in the few days available, if ever.

It was now time for dinner. This was not a social success. Jonathan was showing the early signs of getting 'tetchy', imbibing rather more red wine than was wise, so early in an evening of work, especially when jet lagged, and being openly critical of the Famous Four. Angus and Patrick were skulking at one end of the table, eating in silence and trying desperately not to be noticed whilst Doug somewhat unwisely attempted to engage Jonathan in conversation, concerning the need for better remuneration for the executive team. This was rewarded with a well-chosen volley of expletives from Jonathan, which resulted in a smirk of satisfaction on Ben's face. Monty, meanwhile, was apparently enjoying his food, pausing occasionally to write notes in the little black book that he carried with him.

Eventually, the meal was over and, in an effort to force the Famous Four to interact, Monty decided that their next exercise would be 'cave rescue.'

In this exercise, the participants are supervising the rescue of a group of individuals who are trapped in a cave that is rapidly filling with water. They have to develop a priority list for the rescue as the cave is flooding at such a rate that it is highly unlikely that all can be retrieved before they drown. The teams are provided with biographies of the victims. These turn out to be a Nobel Peace Prize winner dedicated to resolving the Middle East crisis, a lesbian mother of four young children, a leading researcher who is close to developing a cure for Aids, the chief executive of a multinational corporation, a man who is the only form of physical and financial support for his aged infirm parents, and a trades union leader.

Doug immediately refused to take part on the grounds that to make such decisions was to act as God, and that this was against his religious principles. This was strange as one could be forgiven for interpreting Doug's arrogant behaviour as being the direct consequence of him possessing delusions of deity. In fact, it was a total cop out. Despite Monty and Jonathan's attempts at coercion, he could not be swayed, so the exercise was restricted to the other three plus Jonathan. It was not a success; the group could not establish a procedure for prioritising the victims; Patrick's social conscience led to him continuously, but weakly, attempting to demand that the mother and the carer be given absolute priority. This was to little avail as even when he did manage to get a word in, the others were so wrapped up in themselves that they ignored his contribution. To Angus, it was a no-brainer that the Aids researcher and the chief executive must be saved at all costs. Ben looked for clues as to the solution that Monty and Jonathan favoured, and Jonathan, who had done the exercise before, and was only included to make up numbers, became more and more frustrated. Four hours later, long after all the victims would have succumbed to certain death by drowning, Monty called a halt and, with his endless patience, explained how important it was to tackle group decision making in an appropriate manner. This involved letting all contribute, without preconception as to the value of their input, and, most of all, necessitated spending a few minutes at the start of each session jointly setting a few simple ground rules for the process and then sticking to them. This met with blank stares from the participants and yet another derisory snort from Doug who had sat to one side of the group throughout the entire exercise as some sort of self-appointed observer, grunting disapproval as and when he thought fit.

Happily, it was now time for bed and the Famous Four, somewhat relieved that the day was over, skulked off to bed, regrouping with Monty and Jonathan after breakfast the next morning.

Monty's next effort was to try to get the team working in pairs in the desperate hope that this might be a good first stage to integrating the whole team. He was also intent upon having a little fun so he paired Doug with Patrick and Ben with Angus.

One of each pair was blindfolded and the other had to guide him, by means of verbal instruction only, through a maze that Monty had constructed. The pair then had to reverse roles, so that each had a go at each role. Patrick guided Doug through the maze with exemplary, carefully measured, instructions and Doug survived unscathed. Poor Patrick was not so lucky. With similarly precise instruction, Doug propelled him into every conceivable obstruction and he emerged battered and with several cuts to his face. Being Patrick, he merely slunk off into a corner, looking like some injured wildebeest that had just survived a near-death experience with a pride of lions, leaving Doug to gloat complacently at his own success.

Angus took great care to protect Ben from injury, giving unbelievably detailed and terminally boring instruction, to a level that exceeded overkill. Unfortunately, Ben was determined to be faster round the course than anyone else, so failed to listen and ended up in a similar state to Patrick, but was quick to heap the blame for this, somewhat unreasonably, upon poor Angus. Angus, in his turn, went through the maze at a tortuously slow pace like some aged tortoise and, both because of his obsessive need for detail, and Ben's lack of interest, was the only one to seek information from his guide. This was provided sparsely and reluctantly. Thus, another session ended in failure, merely serving to highlight the natural instincts of the individuals and their dislike for each other. Mainly not only to appease Angus by giving him time to catch up with his 'real' work, but also to provide himself with some relief from the turgidity of it all, Monty agreed to call a halt to proceedings until early evening.

It was now time for the team to give feedback on the strengths and weaknesses of one another. Once again, Monty stressed the need for openness and honesty and gave them an hour to prepare, prior to dinner and a modest supply of alcohol. In this exercise, he included Jonathan. Doug and Ben had no difficulty in completing their preparation well within the allotted time, whereas it was clear from his expression, when Monty called a halt, that Angus's comprehensive jottings were far from complete and Patrick was, once again, still staring at a blank sheet of paper. Dinner was a little tense, with Doug, Ben, and Jonathan consoling themselves with liberal quantities of wine whilst Angus and Patrick stuck religiously to iced water. Although the meal appeared to last for an eternity, it was finally at an end and the team repaired to the seminar room to commence the feedback session over coffee, Monty pulling the name of the first victim, Doug, out of the hat, apparently at random.

It is usual in these sessions for the positive feedback to far outweigh the negative, but this looked like an exception. Ben started the feedback, fuelled by an excess of cheap white Zinfandel, by informing Doug that he was a perverted, manipulative, arrogant waste of space with no talent outside the ability to add up a few figures, insinuating that this was well within the capability of any individual not actually challenged by learning difficulties. Patrick mumbled platitudes to the effect that he could see some justification as to why Ben might feel that way, and Angus tried to shore Doug up by saying that, despite these comments he had the potential, if he heeded the feedback, to be a thoroughly nice person. It was now Jonathan's turn to give Doug feedback and he roasted him as totally sham, untrustworthy, hypocritical, narcissistic, and of little value to the organisation. All Monty could do in summing up was to suggest that Doug was a poor fit in the team and needed to review his life goals. Even Doug was wounded by this feedback, which at least tempered his feedback on the others.

Patrick's name was the next to be pulled out of the hat by Monty. Angus was the first to give feedback, dwelling on Patrick's gentle niceness, but suggesting that he should put more energy into directing his sales team, which was, in his view, a shambles. He also alluded to the fact that that he certainly need not get involved in the production area where he was little able to contribute and which was amply covered by Angus and his team. Ben begged to differ, suggesting that both Patrick and himself were well able to contribute to Angus's area and should be encouraged to do so. Ben further encouraged Patrick by saying how much he valued his intellectual input to the team. Somehow, Doug could not be bothered to comment, and Jonathan, already loosing interest in events, limited his input to advising Patrick that he should just get off his f—backside and do something, instead of just talking about it. Monty decided upon the gentle approach, telling Patrick what a wonderful potential he possessed and encouraging him to grasp the opportunity ahead of him.

Angus was next and was initially encouraged by the respect his peers relayed for his ability to get through mountains of toil. He was less encouraged by the feedback that he was secretive, devious, and manipulative. The final blow was when Jonathan told him that he was a complete pain to work with and that he had no idea how to behave as part of a high-level team. Monty immediately saw the crestfallen look on his face and tried to redeem the situation by stressing his ability to get things done and how being more user friendly would complete the package and enable him to flourish within the organisation. It was, however, clear that Angus was severely hurt and that his extreme stubborn streak would inevitably ensure his ultimate demise.

The spotlight then turned upon Ben. The compliments, which were restricted to his intellect and enthusiasm, lasted for all of thirty seconds to be followed by Doug, no longer asleep and keen to retaliate, who waded in to tell Ben that he was shallow, dishonest, and self-opinionated with absolutely no integrity, no financial accountability, and no practical ability. When asked for input, Patrick merely looked the other way, and Angus, still in the early stages of nursing his own feedback, confined his comments upon Ben to suggesting that he should stop meddling in other people's affairs and pay attention to his own. Jonathan, trying to be positive, told him that although he was currently a total failure, he had the ability to be a success, if only he could wake up and direct his undoubted talent to the good of the whole company, rather than to the building of his own empire. Monty attempted to package this better, dwelling on Ben's ability and potential and left Ben in reasonable shape.

Finally, it was Jonathan's turn to receive feedback. Angus started, and, with due deference to authority, presented a list of Jonathan's achievements, confining his criticism to the difficulty of getting enough one-on-one time with him. Patrick stared at Jonathan, again in wildebeest mode, as if about to be eaten by him, and squeaked what he probably believed were his last words, to the effect that it had been nice knowing him and that he hoped they would remain friends in the future.

No fear or inhibitions influenced Doug's oration in which he told Jonathan in unmeasured tones that he may well have succeeded in the United Kingdom, but that this was the States and he didn't even begin to understand American culture or business procedures. He continued by stating that he was foolish not to appreciate Doug's input, especially when it came to remuneration policy. In addition, Jonathan, as head of the organisation was, in his view, undoubtedly guilty of failing to observe most of the tenets of American corporate governance and would, if he had anything to do with it, pay the price for this.

Jonathan sat stone faced through this and thanked Doug for his, for once, sincere feedback. It was now Ben's turn and, being an opportunist as always, he presented a portrait of Jonathan as blending the sort of sainthood demonstrated by Mother Theresa with the business acumen of such legendary business leaders as Jack Welch. This was too much for Doug who muttered something about Jonathan being closer to Ghengis Khan than to either of these visionaries. Even Jonathan couldn't recognise himself as portrayed in Ben's eulogy, much as he might like to, and was, for once lost for words. None of the rest of the team felt it prudent to interject and silence reigned.

By now it was extremely late in the evening, and Monty didn't have the slightest notion as to how he was going to retrieve the situation, so he called a halt and suggested that it was bedtime.

The next morning Monty indulged in his usual pre-breakfast five-mile run and mulled over the events of the last couple of days and, especially those of the previous evening. He knew that he was only an hour or so from conducting the wind-up session, usually designed to send the reinvigorated team home in tip-top condition. Clearly, this was going to be hard, if not impossible, with this group and he resolved to spend one-on-one time with Jonathan to map out this final session and thus, much to Angus's chagrin, delayed the wind up and the group's departure for a couple of hours.

Jonathan was not in good fettle. He was more disillusioned with the Gang of Four than at the start of the week, when he had put all his faith in Monty's ability to achieve what he now in the cold light of day knew to be impossible. Added to this, jet lag had deprived him of all but a vestigial amount of sleep for the whole of his trip and the excesses of the previous night had left him hung over and with acute indigestion, barely consolable with even his liberal doses of antacid. He was thus in fairly 'right-wing' mode when he met up with Monty.

With virtually no exchange of pleasantries, he announced to Monty that as far as he was concerned, the whole Gang of Four should be dismissed forthwith and that, if necessary, he would decamp to Alabama immediately and take over their day-to-day functions as well as the running of the company. After all, this would hardly be a full-time job. With delegation of most of his UK responsibilities, he could easily turn the company around given even a couple of dedicated days per week.

Fortunately, Monty knew Jonathan well and was able to convince him that this may not be the best strategy and urged a more measured approach in which detailed plans should be drawn up over the next week or so and in which the Gang of Four was dismantled on a measured timescale so not as to sabotage the business.

The Gang of Four thus experienced a mixture of surprise and relief when the round-up session turned out to be very mild and short with both Monty and Jonathan stating how useful the week had been and how much better they both understood the team's frustrations. Jonathan then promised that he would be back very soon with plans that addressed these and excused himself announcing, true to type, that he had a plane to catch.

Chapter 12

Up and Away

Although Jonathan was a very seasoned international traveller, the rest of the team involved with our American problem child were, by now, also becoming all too familiar with airlines, airports, and hotels.

In the mid-1980s, leaving Edinburgh by air was a bit like leaving Lark Rise; services were few, and any serious international travel demanded that one first negotiated one of the London airports. Edinburgh's new terminal, which appeared to be huge and empty, echoed to the sound of one's footsteps, and one wondered why such a vast building had replaced the ancient huts that had always appeared adequate to the needs of such a small airport. In hindsight, this is one of the few far-sighted moves that the British Airports Authority has ever managed which, when accompanied by them also building a new runway at ninety degrees to the old one in order to avoid the horrendous cross winds which often closed the old one, was impressive indeed. At the same time, it does lessen one's faith in Britain's armed forces when one realises that the original, constructed as a presumably vital component of our defences, was built in such fashion. Obviously, wars were expected only to be fought in fine weather! Coincidentally, it was not only Scotland's air defences that were handicapped, but also the huge naval dockyard of Rosyth, just a few miles away across the Firth of Forth. This is conveniently located to the landward side of both the mighty Forth bridges, which must represent a handy target to any enemy in time of war!

My own introduction to air travel had been in the early seventies with Derek Thrapp as my travel companion and mentor on a mission to Belgium to inspect European pig breeds (including the somewhat appropriately named Pietrain!). This was not altogether encouraging as Derek prefaced our trip by confessing to a profound dislike of flying and an acute propensity towards airsickness. Fortunately, we both survived the brief flights from London to Brussels and back without mishap although this was, by far, the most successful outcome of the whole trip. Pigs continued to be the reason for all my flying for the next decade as I would sometimes fly to visit Piggy Dick using the wonderful regional airline, Air Anglia that traversed the east coast of England from Norwich to Aberdeen in ancient and noisy Fokker Friendships. The only redeeming grace of this service was the comforting knowledge that Air Anglia had enjoyed an accident free record throughout its entire existence. The route was cleverly designed with a stop at least every two hundred miles—one hour's cruising (which was probably the maximum range) for these machines that jerked and jolted through the sky at such a low altitude that turbulence could be guaranteed. Over each two hundred mile leg, the cabin crew managed to dispense a filled roll and a steaming hot cup of coffee to each passenger. Most of this landed painfully in one's lap, thanks to the turbulence. Boiled sweets were dispensed liberally at take-off and landing to help one's ears, but this was irrelevant as the din of the engines guaranteed deafness for at least an hour after each flight. Most of the airports that the service stopped at, including Edinburgh, had originated as military airfields, and the whole experience was like living out a World War II film, thankfully minus the shrapnel! After these experiences, travelling long haul in 'real' aircraft was almost pleasurable.

The usual routes to Alabama necessitated routing through Gatwick, not easy when rival airlines ensured that the few services from Edinburgh to Gatwick and back ran at the least convenient times possible, with little consideration towards onward connections. In the mid-1980s, Gatwick and Heathrow claimed to be the two largest international airports in the world. This self-awarded accolade is a misleading excuse for their gross inefficiency as, despite their number of international passengers even then, both were dwarfed by many of America's domestic airports. Gatwick truly excelled in being one of the nastiest airports in the Western world. Apart from its appalling design, its carpets with their gaudy, three-dimensional designs were enough to generate a sense of motion sickness in one, even before boarding a plane. How the British Airports Authority (BAA) can still persistently claim that its one runway is entirely adequate for its needs whilst observing the horrendous delays that occur every summer defies logic. In addition, at peak periods of the year, one of the many groups of unionised labour employed by the airport, airlines, and traffic control systems usually conspires to heap further misery on the travelling public by striking for even more money. This is especially harrowing for those attempting to enjoy a cheap package holiday, as many of these leave from Gatwick. To further compound the problem, BAA has crammed every square inch of public space with retail stores. Thus, having been forced to stuff one's personal possessions into one's hold baggage to comply with airline regulations and get through security, one is then invited to occupy the eternity that one usually experiences in the grandly titled 'departure lounge', by purchasing tons of junk to replace it. This is guaranteed to fill all available leg space, once on board, and thus ensure several further hours of misery.

Travelling to America almost always necessitated leaving Edinburgh Airport on the earliest flights of the day. Even with the shorter check-in times of those days, this demanded being at the airport as it opened. With the care so typical of the airline industry in those days (and it hasn't improved much since), none of the shops, restaurants, or lounges at any of the British airports opened to cater for the early morning needs of us passengers, allowing one ample opportunity to fully reflect upon one's current weariness and the long day in prospect. Gatwick practiced a particularly cruel variation of this in the early morning. Having landed at around 6.00 a.m. and cleared immigration, one could walk into one of the restaurants of the absurdly named Gatwick Village and witness a beautifully laid-out, hot breakfast buffet, only to be informed that the restaurant didn't open until 7.00 a.m. Presumably, the fried eggs had to congeal for a while before being judged suitable for serving!

Having arrived at Gatwick, I was usually able to avoid most of this mess by escaping into the hallowed confines of one of the airlines' 'executive lounges'. This is indeed a grand title for any room dedicated to the supply of free coffee and peanuts as solace to those forced to use air travel extensively. It has to be acknowledged that alcohol is usually also available, but who should need the stuff as dawn emerges? The right to use these refuges is dictated by plastic membership cards, categorising one as 'silver', 'gold', 'platinum', or, rather insultingly, merely 'blue' as the lowest form of life recognised in British Airways world (but then what could be expected of an airline soon destined to be run by a man named Ayling, with planning director Ron Muddle and PR spokesman Brian Bashem?). Each colour of card carries a series of benefits concerning which lounges, if any, one can use and on what occasion, nirvana usually being the platinum card, which lets one in any lounge on any occasion. These cards are borne proudly by their owners but should really arouse pity in others and carry the right to free counselling as they testify to the tens of thousands of miles of debilitating air travel and the hundreds of hours endured in airport security and immigration queues by their sad owners. To ensure that privileges are not abused, the airlines guard the portals to their lounges jealously. Indeed, on one occasion, I witnessed a rather snooty British Airways stewardess helpfully cut up an out-of-date card, 'so that you won't make that mistake again,' and send its bearer packing. It is unlikely that he continued to choose to fly 'the world's favourite airline' after that experience!

Our loyalty to individual airlines was fickle, price being the major determinant of choice. This led to some interesting experiences. Whilst the American airlines could, generally, be relied upon to deliver a style of service best described as 'cosy', most European airlines succeeded in delivering a more clinical, even indifferent, form of service. This ranged from the austere but ultra safe Lufthansa to the shambolic Sabena. Indeed, I experienced an all-time low in the latter days of British Caledonian Airways when Sabena and British Caledonian had the inspired idea of a shared service from Brussels to Atlanta via Gatwick, in which British attendants serviced one side of the plane and Belgians the other. This crew demonstrated the difficulties inherent in the concept of a united Europe to the full. The Belgians purposely hid the meals and newspapers from the British! This resulted in one British flight attendant confiding to me that 'that Belgian cow will get my fist in her face in a minute,' this after the Belgian captain had apologised for a delay 'due to the British loaders failing to do their job properly!' It is perhaps a merciful relief for the travelling public, and of no great surprise, that neither of these airlines has survived to the present day.

Once in America, things generally got easier; as long as one had completed the immigration forms correctly, entry to the country was usually easy. Contrary to the warnings given in advance, the immigration staff were extremely tolerant of incorrectly completed forms, although I never had the courage to test their sense of humour by answering the questions, 'Are you a terrorist?' or 'Have you ever committed moral turpitude?' in the affirmative. I have, however, often wondered as to the mental processes of those that construct and approve forms containing such questions. Clearly, terrorists are, at the very least, expected to answer such naively stupid questions with total honesty! The late English writer and broadcaster, Gilbert Harding, of unreliable temperament even when unprovoked, allegedly replied, 'Sole purpose of visit', when challenged with a similar question when applying for a visa to visit the USA. History does not relate whether or not he was granted admittance on that occasion.

Once through immigration, travel to Huntsville in those days usually necessitated travel aboard a four-engine commuter plane. So worn and shabby were the DH 7s that ASA flew that this number of engines was necessary to at least give some degree of hope that we might get to our destination, although the smoke stains around their exhausts suggested that they were far from being in perfect tune—or ran on coal! As with Air Anglia, the din of the propellers guaranteed temporary deafness by the end of the trip. The main qualification for working as a flight attendant on America's regional airlines then and now appears to be the ability to learn the very comprehensive safety briefing by rote and then to recite it at breakneck speed. Maybe competitions are held in this skill. Again the mental processes behind such briefings, which manage to be comprehensive yet incomprehensible, are curious. Surely, a shorter message, concentrating on essentials, and not demonstrating how to latch and unlatch a safety belt, a skill that is well understood by anyone over the age four, would achieve far more!

Whilst all of our many trips were executed in perfect safety, they were certainly not without incident, although our luggage bore the brunt of the mishandling. How it is that American airports can reliably reunite a suitcase with its owner within around fifteen minutes of the plane landing and how they succeed in virtually all instances in ensuring that passenger and luggage follow exactly the same itinerary on the same day is something totally out with the experience and expertise of European airport professionals. The British Airports Authority in particular continues to strive to perfect the art of separating bags from their owners, but why the airlines put up with this and the associated costs year after year is strange, and is a huge service to the travelling public.

Sometimes planes would 'go technical'. This phenomenon is most common on Friday evenings when heading for home! It is encouraging that this almost always happens on the ground before the plane attempts to start its journey, rather than in the air! The first indication, unacknowledged delay, is inevitably followed by an optimistic message from the captain, usually promising regular updates. If these become less and less frequent, and loose their optimism, things are serious and, if it is then decided that dinner will be served whilst on the tarmac, the plane is going nowhere, and the meal is merely a time-filler whilst airline staff desperately seek out beds for the plane's hapless occupants. This has happened to me several times, notably on a Lufthansa flight from Atlanta. In this instance, as midnight approached, we had just begun to endure an exceedingly unpleasant American prepared version of sauerkraut when the captain announced that his beloved aircraft was going nowhere until the next day. The concept of a German flight suffering mechanical failure was so alien to him that he sounded decidedly suicidal. Our night of fun was only just beginning; in an attempt to circumvent the inevitable tedium of being gathered-up and bussed to some remote motel, we opted for the independent approach. Unfortunately, Atlanta was home to a dentist convention that week, and most hotels were totally full of dentists, presumably getting excited over root canals and dental hygiene (or hygienists!). Eventually we found a suitable hotel and hired a cab, which was so low on petrol that the driver spent what seemed like hours, crawling around the suburbs of Atlanta, looking for a 'gas' station, which was open. Eventually we got to our hotel at around 3.00 a.m., armed with the knowledge that we had to be back at the airport by 8.00 a.m., so much for initiative!

Such overnight delays were rare although delays of several hours were more commonplace. This was seldom a problem on the outward journey where one usually managed to be rerouted, thanks to the many available U.S. gateways and their networks of connecting flights. This was certainly made all the more pleasurable by the welcoming nature of American airport staff, which, surprisingly, included the immigration officials. Landing late at Gatwick, usually on a Saturday morning, was a different proposition, guaranteed to involve sacrifice of most of the day or even the weekend to the wonders of Gatwick airport and its staff.

As we travelled more widely in the States, we soon realised that the space and comfort of the Welcome Inn, relative to British hotels were nothing unique. Indeed, it represented the base line for the archetypal American motel. After years of staying in crumbling British hotels with their miniscule and poorly furnished bedrooms, usually with shared bathrooms situated down draughty corridors, it seemed positively luxurious. It came as a surprise that American businessmen, unlike their British counterparts, expected comfortable beds, an en suite bathroom, and room to swing a cat, even in the mid-nineteen eighties. It also came as a surprise that even a single room contained a massive double bed or even two. So much for the English norm of a miserable three-foot wide affair! We soon learnt that age, rather than brand, of motel determined quality, the older ones coming with some interesting extras such as massaging beds where, in exchange for twenty-five cents, one could be lulled to sleep by a feeble, but noisy, trembling of the mattress. Regrettably, an all-too-frequent free extra in such ageing motels was lack of cleanliness and even bed bugs.

As we travelled further from Athens, we realised the rich variety of food that was actually available in America. As we visited customers and contacts, we naturally offered to entertain them at their favourite restaurants, which brought its own problems. It was thus that I became acquainted with barbecue for the first time in an out-of-the-way place in rural Arkansas. This was an experience that I was not enthusiastic to repeat in a hurry due to the immediate onset of indigestion. It has to be said that I was particularly unlucky as barbecue can be quite pleasant to taste, despite its unattractive, shredded appearance. What a way for a pig to end up!

Possibly the most memorable meal-eating experience took place in a steakhouse that was integral with a rodeo ring. Although the show was not taking place at the time, and despite a Perspex barrier between the diners and the horse ring, the smell of horse urine was all pervading and seriously detracted from whatever qualities the steaks possessed. This was my second (and, I hope, final!) experience of dining in the presence of horses. The earlier one had taken place at a function in the stables of a Hungarian hunting lodge. The stables were fully occupied with their permanent equine residents, and we dined in style to the music of a gypsy band. Again, the quality of the food did not compensate at all for the horses and, in this instance, smell was only part of the problem!

CHAPTER 13

AND A TIME FOR PLAY

By now, several of us from Scotland were spending significant amounts of time in Alabama. After our initial deference to the local management's penchant for chauffeuring and chaperoning us all the time, we soon arranged a vehicle and some desperately needed time on our own. This was for at least two reasons. First, and foremost, we needed the opportunity to do the very thing local management dreaded—to plan the future of the business without them, and secondly, we needed a break from their constant company, which was becoming a trifle suffocating.

Prior to having our own vehicle, on one of our early trips, two of us decided that we needed a break from the bland, unwelcoming and alcohol free fare that Athens had to offer. As he dropped us at the Welcome Inn, my colleague, Stuart Aeon, informed Edward Whinning that we wanted a quiet evening on our own and would, on this occasion, forgo his kind invitation to join us for dinner. This both surprised and alarmed me as I had visions of having to survive until morning on the almost inedible fare of the Welcome Inn!

When we were sure that Edward had left, we found the phone number of a Huntsville cab company and set about the challenge of hiring a cab. The first hurdle was the phone system! How did one get an outside line from one's hotel room and arrange for it to be charged to our hotel bill? How did one then get a long-distance line? Why did we need to prefix the number with a '1' (presumably the ever, and nauseatingly, thankful AT&T operator finally realised we were aliens and thus let us into the secret!)?

This resolved that we had to give the taxi company the address of our motel! This we did to their satisfaction, but although they operated from Huntsville airport and whilst Athens, some twenty miles away, was one of the more significant locations in the area, it might as well have been on the moon. Several phone calls from the cab driver ensued before he finally arrived. Stuart, an Aberdonian by birth, told him, in his clearest possible English, that we wished to go to the Fog Cutter's restaurant in Huntsville. After much blank staring and repetition, we perceived a light slowly illuminating somewhere in the cab driver's brain, and he said, 'Oh, you mean The Faaaag Cudder's!' We hastily agreed, and he set off, getting us to the restaurant just before closing time.

Happily, we had retained the contact details of our cab thus ensuring at least the possibility of returning to our motel before daybreak. Taxis are always risky in the southern states. Not only are the vehicles well past their prime, with poorly maintained brakes and steering, but the drivers are, at best, overseas students with little knowledge of the English language or of driving in the United States, probably working nights after a full day of study. At worst, they are well practiced in the use of drugs and alcohol. Despite this, and having several times been tempted to abandon a particularly scary journey, I have thus far always reached my destination without significant mishap.

One of the great mysteries of world travel is the economics of taxi operation. With a virtually captive customer base held hostage to whatever exorbitant charges the local operators choose, why do local standards vary so much? How is it that well-maintained and excellently driven Mercedes are the norm in Germany, whilst in the United States, and even more so in Latin American countries, such as Peru, both cars and drivers lack the bare essentials necessary for the provision of safe and effective transportation? Why also is it necessary for Britain, and more specifically London, to decide that no normal vehicle will meet the needs of the taxicab trade and insist on quaint purpose-built taxis, when this is not an issue in the rest of the world? Britain does, however, score highly in one area—the 'knowledge', the formal examination that prospective taxi drivers there have to pass, which guarantees, however unpleasant they may be, that they know the area that they are licensed to operate in like the proverbial 'back of their hand'. This is far from the case in most

countries and can prove interesting as in Peru, where our driver did not
know the whereabouts of his city's international airport some three miles
from our hotel. This was the least of our worries as he also had little idea
of the concept of driving!

Driving in the United States presents its own challenges. Virtually
all cars are automatic, although once the first fifteen minutes of hitting
the brake hard, in an attempt to depress the clutch and change gear, are
over, one is left wondering why on earth the United Kingdom persists
in favouring the stick shift. The greatest headache to overcome is the
four-way stop. These are commonly situated where two well-used roads
cross and where it would be far more sensible to have traffic lights or a
roundabout. For some unknown reason, these work fairly well, *provided*
that there are no foreign drivers around. Presumably, one gains a huge
respect for these stop signs, usually almost completely hidden from view
in shrubs at the roadside, during one's formative years and even learns not
to be fazed by the random presence, or absence, of road markings at these
junctions! One, apparently, also learns the necessity to stop decidedly at
the sign and not a little further on where one would be afforded a complete
view of the junction. It seems strange that American drivers, otherwise
far more aggressive and discourteous than British drivers, will meekly
stop and take turns in the prescribed manner at these poorly marked
intersections. One can attest to their more normal aggressive state by
merely treating an amber traffic light with the respect it engenders in the
United Kingdom. In the United States, amber is generally interpreted as
an instruction to 'go like hell' before the lights change to red. Any other
strategy leads to much honking of horns, screeching of brakes and verbal
abuse, or worse.

Apart from the four-way stop, one has to learn to cope with the
dreaded school bus. This crude contraption of ancient design, painted
bright yellow and bedecked with so many warning lights that it is more
lit up than a Christmas tree, is supposed to carry children to and from
school in safety. Lacking seat belts and prone to catching fire, even with
a careful driver, its safety is illusory in nature. The best advice to give
anyone not familiar with driving in the USA is to avoid doing so at any
time when they are remotely likely to encounter a loaded school bus!
Failing this, one must be prepared to stop instantly and frequently, as

these busses are prone to stop wherever children live with an eruption of flashing lights and deployment of their built-in stop signs. To pass a bus in such activated state, whichever way one is travelling, is more grievous a crime than murder! The irony of such cocooning of children is that many live in the ever-present danger of the guns and other weapons that are freely available, thanks to the Constitution's 'right to bear arms'. In the light of all the challenges facing the American motorist, it is surprising that Americans find it absolutely impossible to take roundabouts in their stride! These devices, so common in Europe, were only known in a few locations in the USA in the mid-eighties. Indeed, the few that I came across in South Carolina have subsequently required to be severely modified to encourage visiting motorists from the north to use the correct lanes by coaxing them off down exits segregated from the main roundabout by hefty curbs. Despite this, somehow, they manage to get it wrong and cause accidents from time to time.

With very little, if any, instruction, we found ourselves more or less at home on the road, only reminded of our vulnerability by the occasional terrified scream from the odd local, who was brave enough to be our passenger.

The availability of transport and the willingness to drive gave us newfound freedom to explore the area, initially principally to make full use of the opportunity to purchase goods at a fraction of the price one would have paid at home. Even filling the car with petrol, or gas as the locals called it, was a sheer joy as even the thirstiest monster could be refuelled for small change, although Americans were traumatised as the price threatened to exceed $1 per gallon!

Our local meanderings took us around Southern Tennessee and North Alabama. One minute one was visiting the ultimate in high tech, the NASA facility in Huntsville, which helped put man on the moon, the next rural Alabama where the ability to repair basic farm machinery or automobiles appeared to be totally lacking, given the rusty carcases adorning the gardens of most rural homesteads.

An early excitement was the discovery of a bar in the proximity of the office. This building was a few yards across the state line in Tennessee, which was 'wet'. In hindsight, three or four of us visiting in dark suits immediately after work was hugely unwise. Until we spoke, we were probably assumed to be from the Internal Revenue Service or other unwelcome government body. Entry to this drinking den was by squeezing past an ancient pickup truck, sitting on burst tyres, and overflowing with empty beer bottles. Presumably, this was emptied from time to time but certainly not during our lengthy patronage. As we entered to be met by the local clientele, all bearded, missing many teeth, dressed in baseball caps, denim dungarees, and now playing pool in total silence, we observed a purposeful-looking baseball bat in easy reach of the barman. As one of us opened our mouth to order beer, relief spread over all of their faces, and normal conversation resumed; all was clear; we were merely foreigners! In fact, we became semiregulars at 'The Shack' and, despite our outlandish attire, were well accepted.

Apart from being a curiosity to our drinking partners, we certainly were to most of the women that we met. The phrase, 'gee, I sure like your accent,' could be regarded by us as a come-on, especially after many days away from home, but it was usually merely a statement of curiosity. It was intriguing to see how colourful American women were, especially in the workplace. After a lifetime, experiencing the routine drabness exhibited by women in the United Kingdom, it was amazing to see these ladies, day after day, resplendent with attractively tended hair, extensive make-up and bright, well-fitting clothes. Our work attire, usually regulation dark suits, but often not with coordinating accessories, may have merely seemed shabbily quaint, but our lack of casual clothes other than worn-out work clothes must have seemed odd in the extreme.

This was most acute at the various corporate social events. The first that I witnessed was the company picnic, held in the boiling midsummer heat. Here everyone wore extremely casual but new-looking clothing, which contrasted greatly with our tired-looking garments.

The company picnic was unlike any social gathering that I had ever witnessed before. There was an abundance of food and soft drink with monumental quantities of ice. The mainstream events included baseball, a game whose rules are still a mystery to me, and the local temperance band playing discreetly in the background, proclaiming to be delighted to offer their services to any event, provided alcohol was not consumed. They were blissfully unaware that the mellow demeanour that some of us demonstrated was a function of the innocent-looking orange juice that was being dispensed from the boot of the nearby car of the then sales VP, Big George. Big George had, for the last forty or more years, spent Monday to Friday on the road, away from home and living in cheap motels. His only solace and medication was his 'OJ', vodka and orange, the ingredients of which he purchased by the gallon and stored in the boot of his car. Apart from the pleasure of imbibing this, his favourite tipple, he claimed it had afforded him total freedom from coughs and colds. Judging by the undue interest being lavished upon many a parked vehicle, other attendees had made similar arrangements on this occasion!

To the periphery of the main event, various minority sports were in evidence. Horseshoe throwing was certainly worth a look, but the spitting competition, arranged by the most fervent followers of the repulsive habit of tobacco chewing, was well worth taking strenuous effort to avoid. My imperative for doing so had been gained during work time spent with one of the combatants. To observe him, in his office, dribbling the coffee-coloured product of his chewing into a Coke bottle and to view the level slowly rising was merely disturbing, but when in the car and the said bottle became dislodged, spilling its contents far and wide, 'disturbing' didn't come near to describing the effect it had upon me.

The other big social event in the corporate calendar was the Christmas party. This started early in the evening, with a very ample meal, immediately followed by a raffle in which virtually everyone won a prize, which seemed to be the main reason for attending. This was despite the fact that the prizes were universally tacky and of poor quality, condemned to a future of being donated to one charity event after another. The raffle having taken place, the participants evaporated into the night with lightening speed, leaving me to wonder whether the effort of putting on such an occasion could possibly be considered worthwhile or whether I had missed something of significance.

Equally odd to us was to witness the marking of so many seasons in America for the first time. The most reliable indicator is the way the ladies dress, but a restaurant chain, Cracker Barrel, comes a close second. The annual round begins with vengeance in mid-October in time for Halloween. Suddenly the ladies don clothing adorned with images of witches, ghosts, broomsticks, black cats, and other Halloween paraphernalia. This theme is replicated outside most homes. A coup of weeks later, it all changes, and the adornment became turkeys, pumpkins, straw bales, and autumnal leaves. This heralds the start of 'The Holidays'.

The Holidays are a time spreading from Thanksgiving in late November to the day after Christmas, largely regarded as a series of opportunities to eat excessively, although preparation commences a lot earlier than this. During this time, the clothing adornments metamorphose from autumnal to Christmassy. In addition, immediately after Thanksgiving, whole neighbourhoods become filled with outdoor Santas, reindeer, snowmen, polar animals, nativity scenes, and anything Disney has even half thought about. Apart from adorning gardens, these illuminations often dominate the skyline from the rooftops. This is probably the most conspicuous over consumption of electrical energy on the planet, a point that seems to escape the sensitivities of even the most ardent conservationists. One of the mysteries I have yet to resolve is where all these bulky artefacts, and especially the reindeer, hibernate for the rest of the year. Presumably, they go into hiding with Kenny Gee whose music only seems to get airtime at Christmas. Happily for him, it so monopolises the airwaves at that time as to guarantee him a very healthy income. It also helps him and his like that many radio stations dedicate twenty-four hours a day to Christmas music from Thanksgiving to Christmas Day. It is hard to believe that such programming is the result of even rudimentary market surveying.

As with many things, America excels at producing ever more spectacular and, unfortunately, often tackier Christmas ornaments. It's hard to imagine that, in some dark office, an extremely talented electronics engineer is devoting all his waking effort (and probably his dreams) to developing such wonders as sound-activated singing Santas, reindeer, and Christmas trees (complete with moving hands and eyes), all of which, and more have come into existence in the last few years. One can only speculate that the end of the Cold War has led to many such individuals having time on their hands. Still, rather Christmas stars than Star Wars for real, I suppose!

As already intimated, Cracker Barrel sets its own stamp on the seasons, presumably to endorse its own seasonal menu options. As an organisation once, but happily no longer, accused of discriminating against minorities, it can now only be found guilty of targeting one, this time by favouring it. The minority in question is that section of the population, which is addicted to identifying and purchasing all that, is cheap and tacky. For these unfortunates (a clique of which I confess to being a fringe member), Cracker Barrel has an abundance for each season.

The next recognised American pseudo season is Valentine's Day. Again, the ladies decorate themselves, this time with all that is pink and fluffy. Restaurants create special menus, and the shops are filled with sentimentality. After this is Easter with its religious aspect all but replaced by bunnies and chocolate. This seems to end the winter cycle of commercially inspired celebration. Presumably, by this time, the first glimmer of warmer weather is sufficient to ward off depression and lack of consumption, so the retail industry doesn't have to promote additional excess on a national scale.

However, just to be on the safe side, Cracker Barrel does add a few more, celebrating such events as cherry time and apple time, both with their own menus and memorabilia. For some reason, they also have a spell when their shop is filled with a multiplicity of day-to-day objects (mugs, plates, cruet sets, etc.) decorated as if they were Friesian cows. I have never understood why, but on one occasion, this did furnish me with a very appropriate gift.

Visiting rural Arkansas with a business colleague, he, somewhat strangely, introduced a customer to me as 'the cattle pimp of Arkansas'. The customer, Herb, a huge and eminently respectable former football player in his mid-sixties then explained, 'Well, Nigel, when I was a lad, most boys had their first sexual experience with a cow, and my granny had a beautiful little Jersey heifer . . . Problem was that we could only keep her still by feeding her, and granny began to become concerned at the alarming way the cattle cake was disappearing, so I had to collect five cents a time to replace it!'

Shortly after this, I happened into Cracker Barrel and discovered that their 'Friesian' season was in full swing. I spied a Friesian mug with the motif, 'Love me tender, love me true', adorning the rim. I sent it to Herb but never received an acknowledgement!

After all these experiences, I felt dangerously familiar with this country, which many years later was destined to become my home.

CHAPTER 14

ON TRACK AT LAST

Planning is everything, and never more so than to Jonathan on his return to Scotland, following Monty's ill-fated attempt at team building. Instead of turning the Gang of Four into the well-oiled machine that Jonathan had envisioned in one of his most ludicrously optimistic moments, the result of this initiative was worse than his worst nightmare. The immediate future of the American company was now in the hands of a bunch of disillusioned misfits barely functioning as well as rusty clockwork. Once again, Jonathan now realised that he should have listened to his gut and got rid of all four of them months ago, which would have saved a lot of anguish and delay as well as Monty's not inconsiderable fee.

Still, one can only move on from where one is, and Jonathan decided, as always when faced with such a situation, that significant movement had to happen immediately. He, therefore, immediately summonsed those of his senior UK colleagues with U.S. responsibility to an emergency two-day strategy meeting to finally, once and for all, resolve the way forward. As always, Jonathan's agenda was fairly radical, consisting basically of a list of all the U.S. executives with the phrase 'replacement strategy' next to each. The one uniting thread of Jonathan's agenda was its opening item—'secondment of United Kingdom director to United States as company president'. Although uniting, it was only so as long as the poisoned chalice passed to someone other than one's self. Necessity is the mother of invention, and thus everyone in the room had twenty or more excellent reasons why it should not be them, as they were, for the foreseeable future, so urgently needed in the United Kingdom. Finally, this game of 'pass the parcel' ended with the unwelcome package finally landing in Stuart Aeon's lap, much to the relief of everyone else.

Freed from the danger of the imminent possibility of being exiled to America, everyone else felt at liberty to offer bold and irresponsible advice to Stuart on how to run the business. Once he had recovered from the initial shock of his new charge, Stuart took great care to ensure that he would actually have a team to manage when he arrived in the United States and that he would be the one taking the decisions that would determine whether he succeeded or failed over the coming months. All this, in the typical style of Jonathan's meetings, was achieved on the first morning. At lunchtime, Jonathan announced that he was tired after his recent trip, and he went home, not even having the energy to preface his exit with his usual game of golf.

Stuart, on the other hand, tired for exactly the same reason, but possessed by the slowly dawning realisation of his new responsibility plus the challenges of relocation to another continent, was hardly in the mood for rest. He desperately needed to find the time and space to review his entire situation and ensure that he at least had some control over the pace of events.

The one thing that Stuart had little control over was the timing of his departure for the United States and, with scant time to arrange his personal affairs, he found himself at Jonathan's urgent behest on a plane for the United States, some forty-eight hours later. He had little idea as to when he might return home again, but this would largely be at the whim of the American immigration authorities as, even as he travelled, the company's immigration lawyers were drafting the mindless documentation necessary to apply for a work visa.

When Jonathan phoned to tell the Famous Four that he had appointed Stuart, they were joyful. At last, they again had an interface between themselves and Jonathan, and they knew Stuart to be more sympathetic to them and more of a 'people person', which in their minds meant he would be more malleable, or so they thought. Regrettably, for him, Doug had persisted in upsetting certain female members of staff, so much so that the company was facing imminent legal action for failing to deal with the issue in a satisfactory manner. There was only one solution. Doug had to go, and Stuart's first action on arrival in Alabama had to be to resolve this. He was thus left without a VP of finance, but the incident did serve to indicate to others that he was capable of swift action when the need arose, a point that was not lost on the rest of the team, who were on their best behaviour for those first few weeks. Nevertheless, the memories of the week with Monty Steen didn't go away, and Stuart was destined to lose all of them for various reasons over the course of the next couple of years.

Despite the punishing workload involved in turning the company around, Stuart was determined that his domestic base would not remain the Welcome Inn for a second longer than was necessary and thus set about renting an apartment. Much to the consternation of the staff this was, wisely, in Huntsville, not in the backwaters of Athens where, given the desperate nature of many a day's work, suicide may have seemed preferable to the local entertainment available to a lone Scotsman. Soon Stuart found a very acceptable apartment in a gated community in Huntsville and began the process of integration into the local scene; this made all the harder by his punishing workload and frequent travel.

Gated communities in America are similar in concept to the use of black security guards in South Africa, both being designed to lull nonthinking residents into a false sense of well-being. In the American example, entrance to a community, often of many acres, is usually via a single guarded gate or as in the case of the community, which Stuart found himself, an automatic barrier, which can be opened remotely by any occupant (or by anyone else who knows the code). The flaws to such a system are endless. Anyone intent upon entering can usually do so by, at most, scaling a low fence, and the systems are so unreliable that they are generally inoperative. The thought processes behind the implementation of such an arrangement are reminiscent of those behind the construction of a chicken run that I unfortunately encountered, in my youth, in the gardens of a rural rectory where my father did a locum one summer. The worthy rector had built three sides of it so high and so substantial that no chicken could possibly escape but omitted the fourth, hoping, somewhat optimistically, that the woodland in that part of the garden would secure his precious hens. We therefore spent much of our holiday, chasing chickens off the front lawn and back into their run. At the time, I questioned how anyone could be so stupid as to build such an arrangement, but clearly, I was unfairly critical as most of the property developers in America are guilty of similar logic.

The entrance into Stuart's community took the form of a simple plastic arm, which was raised by punching the necessary code into the keypad to let one through. The local pizza delivery boys, infuriated by having their progress impeded for no good reason, took delight in breaking the arm off, and it usually lay forlornly on the ground. Presumably, robbers, mass murderers, and others could use the same technique to gain access.

Despite his efforts at social integration, Stuart came to welcome the visits of his colleagues from the United Kingdom as something of a social lifeline, and thus we came to discover some of the better restaurants and amenities that Huntsville had to offer. At that time, my input into the American company also became very time-consuming and the time I spent with Stuart also helped my integration.

On one of my visits, I was surprised to find that Stuart had joined a local church. Churches and banks in America confuse me, being named in very similar manner to scout and guide troops in the United Kingdom, for example, 'The First Alabama, Church of Christ'. How one sets about choosing a church (or a bank!) remains a mystery. Does one go by the size of the car park, the number of minivans parked outside with the church's name emblazoned on their sides, or the message on the church's roadside display (one of my favourites is still 'What goes up, must come down, Jesus Christ is risen')? It appears that few evangelists can also write scanning prose!

Happily Stuart had been introduced to a small multi-faith church with an extremely modest car park (and no minivans), but a very lively membership. The church was, in many ways, promoting an extension of Monty Steen's message of making the most of one's potential by positive affirmation and lack of self-doubt. The membership both studied widely and had a very active social calendar. When in Huntsville, I would often attend with Stuart and got to know and socialise with his circle of friends.

One evening, a group of us went out to dinner together. I was stuck at one end of the table, finding it difficult to make out the conversation going on at the other, which was being contributed to energetically by a lady, a little younger than me, who was an enthusiastic member of Stuart's church. She seemed, even from my distant vantage point to be both highly attractive and exceptionally interesting, amongst other things having recently completed a parachute jump. I found it sad to learn that she was recovering from surgery for breast cancer, an ordeal that she had faced largely alone, although with the support of a couple of friends from church. She was volunteered to return me to my hotel that evening, and she made it very clear that she had filled her life with work, her family, friends, and church and had no room in it for men. Over the next few months, Mary Ellen attended various events that I was also at, and on each occasion, she made her excuses and left early before I could invite her out.

Finally, one of the ladies of the group, by now a close friend of Stuart and a very good friend of Mary Ellen, decided to throw a party at her house to celebrate Stuart's birthday. Mary Ellen was detailed to pick me up from my hotel and for the two of us to pick up supplies for the party on the way. Despite being very 'English' and underplaying my interest in her, we got on exceptionally well, but only after Jonathan Rampsbeck, a very unlikely Cupid, had, unbeknown to me, attested as to my enthusiasm for her.

The party was an undoubted success and one of the few held by apparently normal forty-year-olds to be visited by police, as neighbours far down the street had complained of the noise. At the end of the party, Mary Ellen took me back to my hotel where we sat and talked in her little sports car for several hours before we bid one another goodnight and goodbye. I was departing for South Africa the next morning and would not return to America for another six weeks. In the meantime, we both agreed to think about whether we should develop our friendship into a more serious relationship, given the major issues of geography and of our respective families.

It is hard to remember how difficult and costly communication was in the mid-1990s. Mobile phones were in their expensive and bulky infancy and tended not to work between adjacent countries, let alone continents. This was, however, irrelevant as I didn't have one, nor could I afford one, especially for international calls. Email had yet to become commonplace, and I knew from bitter experience that the cost of international calls from South Africa was sufficient to bankrupt one. Even from Britain, international calls were seriously expensive. It was thus that I passed one of the longest three weeks I have ever known in South Africa before returning home to Scotland and being able to phone Mary Ellen again, albeit briefly.

It was then a further three weeks before my return to the United States and our agreed meeting to discuss whether or not we had a future.

CHAPTER 15

A CHANGE OF DIRECTION

Nashville airport is a fairly unlikely location for any romantic assignment. Its mainly bland décor is interspersed with more than the odd reference to Nashville's musical heritage, and it features way more hairy, starry-eyed guitar-carrying passengers than is healthy for any airport. It is indeed interesting that, according to its official mission statement, it exists 'to give middle Tennessee its heartbeat and foster its competitive advantage as the region's hub for transportation and related business.' I suppose meeting Mary Ellen there must have constituted 'related business'. One or two of the few underlying values supporting this heady mission are worth a moment:

'Entertaining—our facilities should have a beat and rhythm and exemplify our passion for customer service while being a unique and vibrant place through which to travel.' Regrettably, I have never noticed beat and rhythm in Nashville or any other airport, nor has the word 'entertaining' ever sprung to mind in connection with such a venue.

'Exercising—our most important assets, our employees and facilities, should be kept in top shape. Our employees should have the skills to perform their duties flexibly to meet the highest professional and ethical standards. Our facilities should be optimally managed, made secure, and maintained for their entire life cycle.'

I was totally unaware as to what a lean and mean machine we were engaging with as I stepped off the plane, urgently looking around for Mary Ellen! In those days, security at American airports was virtually non-existent, and anyone and everyone could go to the arrivals gate to meet their nearest and dearest, so I was anticipating that she would be there to greet me. However, she was nowhere to be seen! After a moment's panic, I became aware of her materialising from the depths of the concourse, enthusiastically negotiating her way through the crowds to get to me. She had been delayed by torrential rain on the drive up from Huntsville, but this time, happily I could see that she was certainly making no effort to avoid me, and her amazing appearance belied the fact that she had just negotiated a downpour. Having exchanged cordial but distinctly proper greetings, we made for the baggage hall where, thankfully, my suitcase arrived fresh from its latest dose of assault and battery inflicted at the hands of multiple gangs of international baggage handlers. It was then off to the parking lot and the considerable challenge of squeezing me and my belongings into Mary Ellen's car.

'Practical' is a word seldom, if ever, used to describe the Pontiac Fiero. Apart from a reputation for over-heating, catching fire, and breaking down for a multitude of novel reasons, it suffers from other design features that its small band of aficionados merely find inconvenient. My suitcase just fitted into the miniscule boot (or trunk), which then had to be tied shut with string. This left my briefcase to sit on my lap, wedging me firmly between the seatback and the dashboard. Mary Ellen appeared oblivious to any, and all, of the car's failings. She explained enthusiastically how she was able to transport her aged and frail mother on lengthy journeys, complete with wheelchair, walking frame, and a week's luggage for the two of them plus the inevitable pile of purchases that accrued whenever the two of them were together for more than a few minutes. Besides this, the car was a statement of independence. With her three children now being grown, she no longer needed a practical 'mum's car'. I could understand this, but not in the form of a Fiero, especially this one which went on to fully demonstrate the breed's potential for expensive unreliability as time progressed.

Our brief journey to my hotel for dinner and the much-heralded discussion as to whether we should pursue a deeper relationship was uneventful. On arrival at the hotel, we spent much time getting to know one another considerably better but never found the time for discussion of our future together. This is still the case more than fifteen years later!

The next day, we both had to travel to Huntsville independently, Mary Ellen in the confines of her beloved Fiero, and me basking in the relative luxury and expanse of a very basic hire car. We agreed to meet soon, later the same week. Somehow, the time to this meeting seemed to drag interminably, only alleviated by the bonus of being able to communicate by phone, at length, for virtually nothing. Very shortly after this, I checked out of my motel and into Mary Ellen's very homely apartment, which, although small by American standards, appeared vast to me. This was situated conveniently close to Huntsville airport, actually in Madison County, Alabama.

Thus began the experience of relating to an American girlfriend. The biggest problem was (and still is!) the need to use superlatives when asked such innocent sounding but dangerous questions as 'How do I look?' Almost all of our very few altercations have been initiated by my less-than-overwhelming response to such simple enquiries. This is a very small price to pay, for in all other ways, American custom and practice is far more pleasant and enjoyable than the almost universally drab and straight-laced British equivalent.

All too soon, it was necessary for me to return to Scotland with the associated inconvenience and cost of transatlantic phone calls, which threatened to bankrupt both of us. At this time, I was living in a miniscule and barely furnished one-bedroom flat on the outskirts of Edinburgh, and my return to this lonely garret was particularly distressing, given the stark contrast between it and the warmth of Mary Ellen's home and company that I had just left behind. Fortunately, my work took me away frequently, and I was able to manage the time spent in it between transatlantic trips to an absolute minimum.

From this point on, the 'normal' part of my life was that which I spent in the States where my life was in balance, with a home and social life with Mary Ellen. When not there, I was, almost always, working either in Scotland or in some other part of the world, intent upon filling up as much of my time as possible with business until I could return to Huntsville. It very soon became clear to both of us that we were in love and that this lifestyle was not satisfying to either of us and clearly could not go on for very long if we were to retain our sanity.

It was Mary Ellen who, in her inimitable way, broke first and took the law into her own hands. She resigned her job and announced that she was coming to join me in Scotland, despite my protestations that she should not burn her boats completely until she had at least visited Scotland once or twice to see whether she could stand living in such a climate and with me. Her mother, who never approved of any man in Mary Ellen's life, decided I was wonderful and did everything to encourage her to pursue her new life with me. So she threw caution to the wind, armed with her brand new passport and little else, and returned with me to Scotland at the conclusion of my next American visit.

It is fortunate that, at that stage, neither of us were aware of the various hurdles that governments put in the way of such relationships, the least of which was the initial limit of six months that the immigration clerk, apparently arbitrarily, awarded Mary Ellen as she entered Britain for the first time.

CHAPTER 16

NEW BEGINNINGS

Wisely, as I thought, I decided that Mary Ellen should not be introduced immediately to the grandeur of her new home but that we should first visit one of my favourite parts of Britain, the Lake District. We thus headed south from Glasgow airport on, what seemed to me, to be a fairly pleasant spring day. In hindsight, after Alabama, it probably seemed cold and miserable, but neither of us cared; we were together permanently, or at least for the 180 days that the British immigration authorities had generously allowed.

A couple of hours later, as we left the motorway and travelled ever deeper into the heart of Cumbria, I could see that Mary Ellen was in wonder at the narrowness of the roads and their high density of traffic. She marvelled at the skill of the drivers in not only keeping their vehicles on the road but avoiding those coming towards them as well as an assortment of parked vehicles, hikers, bikers, and stray sheep. The culmination of this occurred as we traversed the Hardknott Pass with its combination of acute vertical and horizontal twists and turns. She absolutely refused to accept this as being a public road. It was at this juncture that I discovered her acute vulnerability to carsickness, something that I find hard to reconcile with her love of roller coaster rides!

My chosen accommodation for this first weekend away together in Britain must have seemed similarly quaint. Being in those days, what my financial advisor somewhat scornfully, but tactfully, referred to as 'cash poor', I had selected a distinctly modest room in a Lakeland pub. The room was located immediately above the bar, thus coming inclusive of much noise as hearty holidaymakers drank and exchanged stories late into the night. Although acceptable by British standards, the room would have seemed minute, crudely furnished, and uncomfortable to any American. Still love conquers everything, and Mary Ellen merely became more and more amazed at the quaintness of her newly adopted country.

The Lake District, uncharacteristically, managed to demonstrate reasonable weather, and Mary Ellen was enchanted by the spectacular scenery with its lakes and mountains, populated at that time of the year by the sheep with their newborn lambs and with yellow daffodils adding colour to an already beautiful landscape. All too soon, our brief visit to The Lakes was over, and we headed north to Edinburgh to introduce Mary Ellen to her new home.

If the lack of space in our room in the Lake District pub was a surprise to her, it was as nothing compared to the diminutive nature of the flat that was to be our first home together. As we approached the group of dull grey buildings wherein my abode nestled, I enthusiastically pointed out the nearby attraction—the Firth of Forth with its road and railway bridges, which was almost visible from my home. This one-bedroom flat, which had been my home for some months, had little to commend it, save cost and the fact that it was modern and easy to keep clean. The décor was stark, the furniture at a minimum and storage space virtually non-existent. This was fine for me, when my occupancy was seldom more than five nights per month, but as our home, in which Mary Ellen could well be incarcerated on her own, for days on end, it was instantly obvious to her that there could be problems. Nevertheless, as she made her first, necessarily brief, inspection, she managed to exude more than weak enthusiasm but instantly set about planning how she could personalise it with the few possessions she had brought with her from the States.

As I was about to travel again on business, I set about the urgent task of familiarising her with driving on the 'wrong' side of the road as she insisted on calling it. My car, small by American standards, but considered large in Britain, appeared huge to her on the British roads and, although I could understand her intense desire not to hit oncoming vehicles, it often seemed certain that this would be at the expense of demolishing the nearside of the car. This was particularly so in urban areas, where she encountered on-street parking, something that is rare on American roads, and only ever if these are excessively wide. Her incredulity peaked when faced with driving on single-track roads, complete with passing places, in the Highlands. What sort of country had she come to live in? Although less than confident that it was a wise thing to do, I left her with the car keys and set off on an overseas trip. Happily, my fears were ungrounded, and she managed to drive perfectly during my absence.

She determined to make good use of her ample spare time and decided that she should get to know Edinburgh. Her chosen method was to drive in a random direction for several miles and then find her way home. As she shunned maps with vehemence (something which she continues to do!), this often took a long time, but she always got home eventually and, within weeks, had a far better awareness for the geography of Edinburgh than I had achieved in over twenty years.

Another way of familiarising herself with her surroundings was to take bus rides. In these early days, mainly in hope of support and information concerning immigration issues, we made contact with the American Women's Association. Through this organisation, we made several good friends but gained little insight, concerning the almost impossibly bureaucratic and hostile process of immigration. These ladies were, however, experts on the complexities of bus travel and could often recite bus routes and times as if by rote. The simple reason for this was that the prospect of driving in Britain, let alone taking the dreaded British driving test appeared to them too impossible to even contemplate. When without a car, and encouraged by these ladies, Mary Ellen thus set forth to discover the bus system and became a rapid convert, marvelling that such a thing existed. Not only did she ride the busses but, much to the surprise of her fellow passengers, attempted to engage them in conversation, a very un-British thing to do and, although tolerated in Scotland, something that could have been to her detriment or even put her in physical danger, further south.

Despite their surprise, once these fellow travellers realised that they were being addressed by an American, their reserve usually melted away. It was thus that Mary Ellen met many who became regular acquaintances and who told her much more about their country and culture than she could ever have gleaned from a guidebook.

As the weeks went by, the imperative of gaining employment became ever greater. This was for several reasons. Firstly, it appeared to be the only way of her staying in the country until I was free to marry her. Secondly, she was supporting her elderly mother, and funds to do so were disappearing fast. In addition, our miniscule flat was hardly the place for a lady of leisure, and she wished to contribute to the community in some way or other.

Gaining interviews was hardly a problem. As commented upon earlier, any American CV compares very favourably with its British equivalent due to the professional and upbeat way in which Americans are taught to present themselves. Mary Ellen was well-qualified for the positions for which she interviewed, and she was very able to present herself at interview. In addition, her bright 'American' appearance comprising attractive, colourful clothes, make-up, and well-tended hair created a very favourable impression. All this was fine, but to gain employment, her potential employer had to demonstrate to the employment authorities that she was uniquely qualified and that, despite exhaustive advertising, there were no suitable British or European candidates for the job.

After many rounds of disappointment, usually due to potential employers either not being willing or able to satisfy this condition, she found suitable employment just as funds, faith, and time were about to run out.

It appears that those involved in writing and implementing the immigration laws of most countries constitute a subspecies of unfriendly, small-minded bureaucrats. They are dedicated to making the immigration process so humiliating, complex, and often, costly, that all but the most determined either give up or take the far simpler illegal route and are then forced to live in fear of instant deportation for the rest of their lives.

Mary Ellen, in possession of a qualifying job offer, had to complete the necessary paperwork in conjunction with her potential employer and then return to a USA address for an indefinite period until the British authorities deigned to mail her a visa to allow her to return to Scotland and take up her new position. Fortunately, all this went smoothly, and she was then able to return to Scotland, secure for three years, always provided she remained in the same job.

Although she loved Scotland, being away from family and friends was tough, especially in the early months and on American public holidays, which are traditionally times when families get together. Her first July 4 (America's Independence Day) was not an outstanding success. We joined the American Women's Association for their traditional Independence Day picnic. Gathering on a dull Edinburgh July day, without the American ball games, knowing very few of our fellow picnickers, and with Mary Ellen thousands of miles from her family, she felt extremely far away from home.

By then it was necessary to introduce her to my parents, now retired to the Lark Rise cottage that had formerly been occupied by 'Mandy' Needham Davis and her husband. This was fraught with risk. My father disapproved of Americans almost as violently as he disapproved of divorce; Mary Ellen was qualified for his disapproval on both counts. The phone call to arrange the visit went surprisingly well, probably, I thought, because my mother, who could never think badly of anyone, answered the call, even enquiring whether we required one bedroom or two. Despite my being close to fifty years old, this degree of consideration came as something of a pleasant surprise.

The four-hundred mile journey south seemed interminably long and the hours filled with all manner of concerns, but within minutes of our arrival, Mary Ellen had made firm friends of both of them and, especially, my father. They discovered they had common interests, not only as avid gardeners, but also in the hospice movement and, provided Mary Ellen put down her gardening gloves early in the evening and joined him in a glass of his favourite claret, which he assured her was 'French, of course; none of this New World muck!'; they got on famously.

My mother put on her traditional generous spread of food. Even in her younger days, her offerings verged upon the hazardous, and as she became older, they certainly didn't improve!

The war years had imprinted on her mind the imperative of avoiding waste. The 'best before' dates on the food in her refrigerator were taken by her as a challenge and certainly did not merit serious scrutiny by anyone of a weak constitution. Woe betides anyone who pointed out the vintage of any item. Cooking was a challenge due to the poor condition of the cooker and lack of space in her kitchen. Neither of these features was by design. During her life, she had many new stoves, each of which she managed to reduce to scrap within months, so much so that a 56 lb weight balanced precariously on an upturned saucepan served to secure the door of her various ovens for many years. The lack of space in the kitchen was due to the multiplicity of discarded plastic tubs and tin cans that decorated every horizontal surface, the contents of each destined either for a charity (aluminium or plastic) or to feed a particular animal. Scraps from each meal, once beyond human consumption, were allocated on some basis that only she knew, and which didn't exclude cannibalism to feed the dog, cats, geese, chickens, and ducks.

The main meals on this occasion were, predictably, fish pie, which was safe except for bones and its degree of carbonisation, and roast beef, which, this time, was seriously rare but which could just as easily been 'done to death' as a previous example had once been described. Deserts were similarly predictable. Apple pie, with her own twist, the connective tissue from the centre of the core (happily minus pips) was the main feature. Finding these shards in a mouthful of otherwise pleasant pie was like chewing on toenail clippings and definitely best avoided. Another staple, with which Mary Ellen was presented, was crème caramel. I have never met my mother's favoured variety anywhere else and can only describe it as 'industrial grade', having the consistency of lumpy porridge with the caramel sauce and the colour and flavour of tar.

Mary Ellen coped better than most with these offerings, only having real difficulty with the steak and kidney pie, its antiqued pastry crust hiding beneath it, the offal of which my mother was so fond. It came as no surprise that, despite our less-than-abundant financial situation, enthusiastic suggestions that we should treat my parents to a meal out were frequent!

Both my parents were by then beginning to decline. My mother, never one to complain, had fallen down the church steps some years earlier and never sought medical help. This was probably the start of a hip problem, which left her in continuous pain. Added to this, but largely masked by my father, she was beginning to suffer from Alzheimer's disease. My father, outwardly still extremely positive, was supporting her, but he himself was beginning to fail and was unable to maintain their beloved garden. It was thus that we determined to be frequent visitors and to ensure that the house and garden didn't get beyond them.

CHAPTER 17

CONSOLIDATION

As time progressed, Stuart Aeon's determination and focussed effort began to pay off. With capable managers now in most positions, the fortunes of the company began to improve, and the challenges of successful growth began to occupy his days, rather than the previous tedium of sorting out the battles between the Gang of Four.

Jonathan Rampsbeck, as always, anticipated the emerging need long before action was actually necessary, which could be highly frustrating. Stuart frequently said that, in times of extreme workload, which were many, Jonathan would try to rescue him by 'throwing him a concrete life-raft', guaranteed to finally sink him! This was further compounded by Jonathan's genuine offers of help, which Stuart knew, from experience, would divert his own purpose and involve him in even more toil!

It became imperative to relocate the American office, which now comprised three buildings, all located in the same rural Alabama backwater that the company had occupied since my first visit.

Even in the early days, Jonathan had asked Edward Whinning to have a 'clean sheet, no constraints' look at where the office would ideally be located, given the company's customer base. His report, running to over fifty pages, listed dozens of reasons for leaving it exactly where it was and not even one for its relocation. It may be pure coincidence that Edward had recently purchased a house within two miles of the office!

Stuart, quite rapidly, came to the obvious conclusion that the optimum location was Huntsville. Huntsville had such novelties as an airport, nice hotels, and excellent restaurants, all of which made the experience for visiting customers all the more enjoyable than the dubious delight of the Welcome Inn! In addition, the availability of skilled staff was much greater in this thriving city.

It was perhaps inevitable that a significant number of staff chose not to commute to the new location, which was some forty-five miles from the old. This was ultimately a blessing, although it did not appear so at the beginning. At the old office, the number of individuals related to one another was huge, which could cause problems if one member of the family became at odds with the organisation. Also, this being an exceedingly rural location, one UK executive suggested that, were we to stay, we would have to tap the 'granny generation' to recruit further staff!

Another advantage of Huntsville was that there was an abundance of office buildings for rent. Whilst selecting a suitable building, Stuart turned his attention to office furniture. Always wishing to appear 'leading edge', he arranged for a visit to a manufacturer of futuristic office furniture.

The premise of this organisation's offering was the provision of different facilities for different functions. Thus, for thinking, one should reserve a 'think pod', which had the external appearance of one of those terrifying-looking modern coin-operated public lavatories as situated on the streets of London and other European cities. In those pre-laptop days, there were also computer workstations, of minute dimensions, cellular offices for one-on-one meetings, and other designs for meetings of various sizes. Each employee was to be provided with a file cart, about half the size of a conventional file drawer, which had to accommodate, not only one's files, but also all the other personal bits and bobs that one usually stores in and on one's desk. Each night, one of the hapless employees was expected to wheel their file cart to the 'cart garage' and lock it in its personal space. The cart obviously deserved its dedicated space, but the employee did not!

Not only did this system run counter to everything known about human psychology in terms of one's personal need to have an office space, however small, which can be called home and be personalised with family photos, etc, but it must have been a logistical nightmare to manage for any company crazy enough to have it installed. How many people know how much time they will spend thinking tomorrow, how many think pods does an organisation need, and what happens if these are oversubscribed on a particular day? In addition, this was before the days of mobile phones, so programming of the office phone system to keep up with the ever-changing locations of the workforce must have been a full-time job. After the enthusiastic salesman had extolled the wonders of the system, Jonathan, on his best behaviour for Stuart's sake, made the apparently innocent statement, 'I have a slightly different point of view.' Those of us who knew him well winced inwardly, knowing that he was about to reduce the salesman's presentation to ashes, which he did! Needless to say, the new office was furnished in traditional open plan style!

Moving into the new office had many unexpected benefits, staff could actually visit the adjacent shopping mall in their lunch hour and, therefore, save a huge amount of their weekends or evenings that would previously have been wasted on this routine chore. Going out to lunch no longer meant settling for the one very basic establishment down the road from the old office or driving for at least fifteen minutes to get to the plethora of fast food grease palaces that Athens offered!

As far as the business was concerned, the offices and their location, not only impressed visiting clients but was efficient. From the time of this move, the company began to grow, largely thanks to Stuart's leadership and the refreshing professionalism of the team that he had recruited. The problems that we now encountered were those of a successful, growing, company rather than dealing with lunacy; a refreshing change indeed!

CHAPTER 18

LARK RISE REVISITED

Visiting Lark Rise with Mary Ellen every few weeks, I rapidly renewed my acquaintance with the village that had been home to the family many years' previous. This was not a lengthy process as little had changed. The village school and the local pub had closed down, and both were now private houses as were several of the farm buildings. The saddest change of all was that a neat line of headstones in the churchyard now represented most of the stalwarts of my father's congregation from our earlier days.

Although Lark Rise was virtually unchanged, this was not the case with nearby Brackley. Despite the heavy through traffic now having been relieved by a bypass, there had been so much messing about with the once spacious market square that it was now nearly impossible to find a parking space within it, and Brackley still felt congested.

Magdalen college school, now part of an unwieldy amalgam of all the secondary schools in the town, had become some form of Sixth Form College with its trendy maths and computer-learning centre. Eric Forrester, the bellicose tyrant who had blighted the life of so many pupils during his seemingly eternal reign, which included my year as a pupil, must have been spinning in his grave as crocodiles of scruffy youths of indeterminate sex, clad in tired jeans and other shabby garments, traversed the town to attend lessons at one or other of the sites that had once been separate schools. Even back in the sixties, the minor dress code infringements of pupils from the Girl's High School had necessitated him labelling them as 'second rate tarts' from the pulpit of the school chapel. Heaven only knows how he would have tagged the current generation of students in their untidy choice of clothing.

British Rail had long ago forsaken Brackley, and the station from which I had set forth in my school days was now gone, replaced by a so-called 'executive' housing estate comprised of many small, unimaginative box-like homes, unlikely even to appeal to those beginning to climb the greasy pole to executive nirvana. Many local businesses had disappeared; Eric Swan's garage, once a proud outlet for the essence of the British motor industry, Austin and Morris, had been transformed into a beauty salon, this after a brief spell of ignominy as a Skoda dealership. The local food retailers had largely succumbed to the pressures of a Tesco superstore, the agricultural merchant had moved out, and much of the void in the town centre had been taken up by a plethora of gift shops, coffee shops, and other non-essential tourist trivia. Even the private house that had served as my lodgings for a short while had not escaped change and was now a dusty second-hand bookshop.

Back in Lark Rise, my parents had settled into a contented routine of retirement. Upon retirement, my father had felt it imperative that he had a comfortable study from which to contemplate the world and within which to smoke his pipe profusely. The first thing that he had to do was to construct monstrous bookshelves along the longest wall. This he did in his practiced manner, ensuring that they were such a tight-fit as to stay in place without resorting to the unknown (to him) art of plugging the wall. He then loaded the shelves with his extensive and weighty devotional library, comprised, in equal parts, of theological texts and World War II paperbacks. Even his courage failed when, whilst standing back to admire the neatly arranged collection, he reached for a chosen text and the whole edifice swayed like a drunken sailor. It was thus that he sought professional help to tether his handiwork to the wall, thus averting certain injury or worse. Having housed his library, he then placed his desk, complete with vintage typewriter, in the window. He was thus able to observe village life as it passed by on the main road. Regrettably, there was little traffic to observe and, as time went on, the frequency with which one of the regulars, the postman, actually stopped to deliver anything dropped dramatically.

To redress this situation, my father became an avid subscriber to the *Reader's Digest*, thus guaranteeing an almost daily flow of correspondence. This largely consisted of intimations that he was through to the final round of their latest competition and that he was virtually guaranteed to win a life-changing amount of money. Of course, linked to this was the rider that his chances would improve immeasurably, should he choose to purchase one or more of their exciting array of books. It was thus that the whole family received *Readers' Digest* publications every Christmas and birthday for the rest of his life. It was only after his death that the serious side of this came to light as witnessed by the bizarre array of books and tapes that we found in his study. There were books on exercise and healthy eating (where any interest he entertained was purely theoretical), a book on crochet (useless to my mother who was virtually blind), and a comprehensive collection of Crystal Gayle tapes, the reason for which I couldn't even guess. I believe that he was typical of thousands of intelligent, elderly people who are, to this day, preyed upon by such organisations, which exploit their frailty and feed their desire for greater financial security.

My father was much in demand to take Sunday services at the many country churches that were without a permanent priest. Despite having visited most of the villages in the area many times, he would insist on a midweek 'recce' to check that the church he was to officiate at on the forthcoming Sunday had not moved (all of them had been built in the Middle Ages!), had not been isolated by a new bypass (this was quite possible!), and that there was ample parking (never a problem, given the size of their Sunday congregations!). All this was, of course, a patently transparent ruse to coax my mother out of the house and ensure himself of at least one excellent lunch each week at one of Oxfordshire's ample stock of village pubs. My father's chosen meal always had one essential feature—a total lack of any green accompaniment. In his retirement, he had decided to eschew any green vegetable or salad item. The reason for this was unclear although it was a step certainly not calculated to improve his health, but woe betides any hapless waiter or waitress that ignored his specific instruction on this matter!

As time passed, my parents relied more and more on our visits to keep their cottage garden under control although my father never conceded that his more radical ambitions for landscaping were now beyond his physical ability. Our weekends of gardening and household repair were constrained by the 6.00 p.m. curfew imposed by my father as, at this hour, he would open a bottle of his favourite French claret and demand that we sit down and enjoy it with him. Meanwhile, my mother, possibly consenting to a small sherry (of which she was unlikely to consume more than a sip) would prepare dinner, hopefully, coming up with something that was not likely to prove microbially challenging to us and that was possibly edible! Food apart, these evenings were always enjoyable and contributed to the growing bond between Mary Ellen and my parents.

Soon I was free to marry Mary Ellen, and we arranged to fly my parents up to Edinburgh for our simple wedding ceremony in the local registry office. Although my father's unswerving and extremely conservative loyalty to his church did not allow him to marry us, something of my parents' joy at our marriage was evident in the poem that he composed as a reply to our invitation:

> Your invitation we accept,
> With thankfulness and glee.
> To Edinburgh we bring ourselves,
> And tread most thankfully.
> Francis and Mary Ellen'll be there,
> With Jenny and Mark as well.
> This Marriage will show
> How much we care.
> What a fairy tale to tell!

This visit to our home in Edinburgh turned out to be their last. Our next visit to Lark Rise was for a service of blessing upon our marriage held in Lark Rise church with the whole family, numbering nearly thirty, and comprised of rather more children than my father would normally feel comfortable. Mary Ellen promised to keep them seated in the pews, and the service followed his chosen form of restrained joy, the ebullience of the children being capped until after the service when, with Mary Ellen's encouragement, they gave full vent to their excitement.

We followed this with a wedding blessing on our favourite mountain in Huntsville. Mary Ellen's mother, children, and many dear friends were attendants, all showing much joy and support for this long-awaited union.

Shortly after these celebrations, my mother went into hospital for her much-anticipated hip replacement. Unfortunately, the onset of Alzheimer's, which had been hidden by my father but which had certainly not improved her cooking skills, became readily apparent, and it was evident that she could never return to Lark Rise. Facing up to this, my father's health declined rapidly, initially in the form of collapsed vertebra (not helped by his shunning of vitamin and calcium-rich vegetables).

Ultimately, he lost the will to live, knowing that life with my mother was, essentially, over, and he died in hospital some months later. One of the disadvantages of being a priest in this situation must be to awake, in one's hospital bed, to discover that one is surrounded by a gaggle of solemn-looking clerics. This must tell one, even stronger than the distinct feeling of unwellness, that the game is up. He was buried in his beloved Lark Rise, joining his ex-parishioners in the neat line-up in the churchyard.

Emptying a family home, following such a course of events, is a sobering experience. The contents, representing a lifetime of accumulated possessions and memories, less the inevitable dust and decay occasioned by the onset of old age, hardly do justice to the souls that lived there. Nevertheless, the process has to be carried out, and thus my brother and sisters joined us in the task. As we cleared the house, the contents rekindled old memories and surprisingly resulted in much happy laughter. In addition, we will remember forever the number of places around the house in which my mother had secreted new pairs of tights. Her illness, plus her wartime-induced habit of hoarding, had led her to hide tights in every room in the house. My father's hoarding of unwanted items was largely restricted to his heap of *Readers' Digest* books and tapes waiting for a suitable gift opportunity, although his study contained a fascinating collection of items marking various steps of his life.

Thus the family's second occupation of Lark Rise came to an end in the form of a couple of van loads of furnishings and a bonfire that lasted for days. Mary Ellen and I were in the process of purchasing a larger home, which resulted in at least some of the furniture with which I had grown up, finding a new permanent home within the family.

This period also marked Mary Ellen's emotional acceptance of the United Kingdom as her home. This happened in parallel with the formal process of obtaining permission for her to live permanently in the United Kingdom, without fear of deportation if she lost her job. Once again, we had to approach the immigration authorities, this time in their unfriendly offices at Glasgow airport. It would be easy to assume that current marriage to a British national would be sufficient qualification to allow one to stay in Britain, but this is far from the case. Indeed, a friend having married her British husband and then immediately left the country with him to work overseas for two years, found herself summarily deported at two weeks' notice and told to apply from her home country, when attempting to return with him some two years later! We were mercifully spared this sort of insanity, but I had to prove that I was capable of supporting Mary Ellen before she was granted the unimpressive permanent residence stamp in her passport. What happens to any impoverished unfortunate who happens to fall in love with a foreigner? I dread to think.

Thus our life together gained a sense of permanence, being together was no longer at the arbitrary whim of an employer or government, and we were able to concentrate on living our lives to the full. The ageing of my parents, and the death of my father, had facilitated Mary Ellen's being accepted as a full member of my family and bound us even more strongly together.

We continue to be blessed with five wonderful children between us, wonderful friends, and a life that is happier than either of us could have imagined in our younger years.

LaVergne, TN USA
17 November 2010
205295LV00002B/4/P